MAXIMUM MARRIAGE

TIM TIMMONS

Fleming H. Revell Company
Old Tappan, New Jersey

Scripture quotations are from the New American Standard Bible, Copyright © THE LOCKMAN FOUNDATION 1960, 1962, 1963, 1968, 1971, 1972, 1973 and are used by permission.

The principles in *Maximum Marriage* are essentially from the Christian Family Life Seminar. Cartoons and diagrams are from the Christian Family Life Seminar manual and are used by permission.

Library of Congress Cataloging in Publication Data

Timmons, Tim.
    Maximum marriage.

    1. Marriage. I. Title.
BV835.T55   301.42'7   76-10746
ISBN 0-8007-0801-6
ISBN 0-8007-5003-9 Power qpb

MAXIMUM MARRIAGE

Contents

Foreword

"Don't curse the darkness, light some lights!"

Despite the secular prophets' relegation of marriage to the obituary column, the institution of marriage is alive and well. It is not marriage that fails, but people. People fail because they build their lives and relationships around blueprints of human origin. God is the magnetic north pole of marriage. He is the fuel of the human spirit, the Designer of the marital relationship. If God designed it, He should be able to make it work.

God's power works best in cemeteries. Many marriages have reached a stage of "living death" and desperately need the fresh wind of the Spirit to bring vitality and beauty. Tim Timmons charts a pilgrimage toward maximum marriage which invites us, not to try harder, but to look closer.

Change comes by reconstructing new mental images of the person I am to be. "As a man thinks within himself, so he is" (*see* Proverbs 23:7). Tim Timmons skillfully paints a picture of the biblical "game plan for marriage" which puts the truth where it hurts. Tim's extensive counseling and speaking experience puts him out of the realm of being an "armchair theorist." His writing will make you feel someone has been eavesdropping on your marriage. Step by step he leads the reader through the *Why* of marriage, the commitments which make it work, and the practical steps toward implementing the divine blueprint.

With his characteristic light touch, he has spelled out the all-important *How* with balance, realism, and practicality. This book will be used to bring beauty and wholeness to many marriages.

H. HENDRICKS

Introduction

"All weddings are happy; it's the living together afterwards that causes all the trouble." When all the sparkle and glamor of that beautiful day wear off, a period of living together begins. Various clichés are used to describe marriage. Some jokingly say: "Marriage is a cafeteria—you take what looks good to you now and pay for it later." Or "Marriage is an adventure—like going off to war!" "After all, if it weren't for marriage husbands and wives would have to fight with strangers!" Others offer advice of a more serious nature: "It's a fifty-fifty proposition." Or "You must give and take in marriage."

Each of these tidbits of advice falls far short when it comes to describing the actual nitty-gritty of living together. Today there are too many homes being broken up by divorce. Even more tragic than the divorce rate is the incredible number of so-called marriages that are nothing more than a living "divorce." These homes are full of disappointment, resentment, and a spirit of enduring rather than enjoying the marriage. It isn't that each of the partners doesn't want to make things work out for the best. On the contrary, from the beginning each person has sought and expected the very best of the marriage relationship. But as each one seeks total fulfillment and full expression of himself he meets failure and disappointment. So he gives up. Then the man and the woman find themselves caught up in a marriage where all of their expectations for happiness are disintegrating before them. No, it isn't a lack of the "want to," but a lack of the "hope" that it could be any better. This process of disintegration is what I call *Plan A.*

Plan A

Plan A is the most popular plan for marriages today. It follows the familiar advice "It'll all work out!" and it usually does, but not the way you would like.

Plan A is based upon competition and comparison—constantly asking the question "Who is more qualified, the man or the woman?" As each person sets out to answer this question he is thrust into a power struggle to prove himself more qualified than the other. When Plan A shifts into full operation, the marriage moves down the road to disappointment and despair. Plan A does not work! And yet many, if not most, homes today are operating to some degree within Plan A. In order to capture a full description of the operation of Plan A let's take a look at each family member in the process of disintegration.

Man

1. *Reasons from confusion*   The man has heard that he is expected to be the *head* of his home—whatever that means. But when he asks himself the question, Who is more qualified? he responds: *Well, I certainly am in many areas; but then again, my wife is more qualified in quite a few strategic areas.* Here is a man who misunderstands *headship* and feels bound to answer the magic question, Who is more qualified? This is the kind of man who is continually feeling the need to announce himself as "the head." He comes home and says, "I am the head!" His wife doesn't believe him. Nobody else in the home votes for him, so he retreats.

2. *Retreats from responsibility*   Without a clear understanding of *how* he is to function within the framework of the home, the man begins to retreat from his responsibility. His normal theme song is, "I'll take care of the office—you take care of the home."

3. *Resents his wife*   Once the man removes himself from active responsibility within the home he sits back in his critic chair. From this vantage point resentment builds toward his wife

for taking over in various family matters and decisions. This is the same man who retreated from responsibility but now is filled with resentment toward his wife.

4. *Reacts against his wife*   The resentment the man has for his wife surfaces in frequent confrontations; he tries to prove himself more qualified than his mate by pointing out where she's "blown it." Usually he'll say, "If you had only consulted with me, this problem wouldn't have come up!" This kind of reaction is nothing more than the deadlock of competition and comparison found within Plan A.

5. *Runs elsewhere*   He's seeking total fulfillment and full expression of himself as a person but hasn't found it at home. So he runs elsewhere. The man normally runs to his business. At least there he finds a thread of respect, appreciation, and full expression of himself. The man may run to some kind of sport (tennis, golf, hunting, . . .) or social organizations (clubs, men's groups) where he continues his search. Some men even run to another woman—one who will truly listen to him and build him up. Any one of these can be a poor substitute for a maximum relationship with his wife.

Woman

1. *Reasons from pride*   The woman follows the same pattern as the man. Instead of starting from confusion, she begins from pride. You see she has heard that she is to be the helpmate in her home. To her, *helpmate* along with the "dirty" word *submission* is equal to *doormat*. Because of this misunderstanding of her function in the home, she is out to prove herself more qualified than a doormat. So when she asks herself the question, Who is more qualified—the man or the woman? her natural response is: *Well, I am in many areas. Besides,* she thinks, *if I don't do it, it'll never get done!*

2. *Releases her husband from responsibility*   In her energetic effort to outdo her husband and prove herself she subconsciously pushes her husband out of meaningful involvement in the affairs of the home. She doesn't encourage him to take his responsibility as head of the home because her definition of

headship is summed up in the word *dictator*. Obviously, this is diametrically opposed to her showing herself as more qualified than her husband.

3. *Resents her husband*   Although she released her husband from his responsibility in the home, she begins to feel resentment toward him. She comes to the realization that she did not get a very good deal in the Plan A arrangement of the home. The woman is weighed down with the pressures of coordinating the activities of the home, the discipline of the children, the cooking of the meals, and the cleaning of the house. On top of all this incredible amount of unappreciated work she discovers that she is desperately alone! So she resents her husband and his thoughts, opinions, and activities.

4. *Reacts against her husband*   She, too, begins to lash out against her mate because of her resentment of him. The familiar reaction to a crisis situation is, "If you had only been the man of the house this would not have happened!" The power struggle is on! The spirit of competition and comparison permeates the atmosphere of the home!

5. *Runs elsewhere*   She's seeking total fulfillment and full expression of herself as a person, but hasn't found it at home. So she runs elsewhere. The woman normally runs to her children at first. This provides some kind of relationship for a time, but children grow up and become independent of the parents. She then runs to women's organizations or a vocation. There is nothing wrong with any of these activities in themselves, but when they become replacements for a relationship with her husband, they tend to increase the cold chasm between husband and wife. Some women run toward other men; they seek someone who will offer a breath of appreciation, understanding, and respect—someone who will care and treat them like a valuable human being.

Do you see what is happening in the Plan A home? Nobody's home! You can phone them night and day, but no one will answer. Everyone is running away! This sets up one of the most tragic scenes in our society today—the development of the child within a Plan A home.

Child

1. *Reasons from insecurity*   The child's basic security factor is not derived from the fact that his mother and father love him, but that his mother and father are warmly excited about one another. However, within the Plan A home the parents just don't have this kind of relationship. Instead of receiving strength and security from his parents, he is caught up in the spirit of competition and comparison along with his parents.

2. *Refuses to communicate*   There is a natural shift in the development of a child from dependence to independence. In order to survive this shift with relatively few explosions the parent-child relationship must be healthy and warm. Within Plan A this shift is met with a cold system of rules. The child responds to this system by retreating in order to create and live in a world all of his own which excludes his parents. Communication lines between parent and child only open up for necessary interaction. The real child—with his interests, thoughts, and feelings—gradually becomes concealed from the parent.

3. *Resents his parents*   The child begins to face life alone. His relationship with his parents is disintegrating. The most natural source of security and strength has been cut off. The result? Resentment builds toward his parents! "They just don't understand!"

4. *Rebels against his parents*   By this time the child experiences enough of Plan A through observing his parents and he joins the power struggle. Again, the parents respond with more restrictions; but restrictions, without a relationship, cause rebellion every time. Now he's out to prove something. "I'm not too young! I know what I'm doing!"

A mother asked me concerning her fourteen-year-old son, "What can I do about my baby? He's been so rebellious lately." It didn't take a lot of insight to discern the problem here. I responded, "You might begin by dropping *baby* from your vocabulary." "Oh, but he's our baby!" On his sixteenth birthday he obtained his driver's license, took the car out on his first drive alone, and returned drunk. Obviously, he was trying to prove something: "I'm not a baby!"

5. *Runs elsewhere*   The child was meant to find total fulfillment and full expression of himself as a person within the family unit. Instead, he must search outside the home. He finds himself at the mercy of his peers. It's at this point that the child is surrounded by strong social and emotional pressures to *experiment with* or *try* different things for acceptance. These experiences can be very unhealthy, defeating, and sometimes damaging for the child, because he has no secure base from which to step out into the world.

One of the most tragic effects upon children within the Plan A home is the problem of homosexuality. In a book highly endorsed by the National Institutes of Health *Growing Up Straight,* Peter Wyden reveals that "research findings overwhelmingly indicate that homosexuals are not born but bred . . . there is increasing agreement that homosexuals rarely (if ever) occur without some important (or controlling) contribution from parents . . . . Many parents underestimate their own importance as models for the behavior of their children, especially while the children are still young . . . . They should appreciate that a mother's acceptance of her role as a truly feminine woman will communicate itself to a daughter at a remarkably early age; and that a mother's respect for the father's role as head of the family will help a small boy grow up to be masculine. On the other hand, if parents themselves are unsure about what constitutes appropriate male and female behavior today—or, especially, if they are competitive with each other—their children are bound to become confused about their place in the scheme of things." This is not to say that all Plan A homes will produce homosexual children. However, it is saying that all homosexual children are produced in Plan A homes.

Plan A is filled with heartache because everyone loses. The child has lost a secure base from which to step out into the world; and the parents, for all practical purposes, have lost their child.

Plan A does not work! It leads to despair and disappointment.

Plan B

What we need is a plan full of hope for living together in marital oneness—a plan for *Maximum Marriage*. *It must be a game plan for marriage which provides for total fulfillment and full expression for the man and the woman—as individuals and as partners* within a dynamic oneness *of the marital relationship.*

Search the libraries of the world for such a plan. You can find advice for fighting things out, advice for contractual marriage, advice for friendly competition, and even advice on how to cope with extramarital relationships. Most of these suggestions are insightful and even temporarily helpful. But this advice doesn't offer an absolute plan or strategy for oneness.

There is only one plan for marital oneness in existence today. It was written centuries ago by a few Jewish prophets and teachers and over a period of fifteen hundred years. These men, inspired by God, were expressing God's design for man in this world. In it can be found the plan for living together within the family unit. Some would find it strange that the Bible, written so long ago and in a different culture, could have anything relevant for our family life today. Even Christians, who are more sympathetic to the Bible, tend to expect nothing more than some theoretical jargon concerning the marital relationship. I find more people shocked over the Bible's practical and positive application within the complexity of the twentieth-century home. This plan for marriage is basically summed up in the equation: one + one = one. It's an exciting process of the man and the woman growing toward a vital, intimate relationship. We'll call it *Plan B*. *Maximum Marriage* sets forth the definition, operational principles, and illustrations of Plan B.

The foundation of this exciting plan is given in Part One, "Competition or Completion?" God created the earth and said, "This is good!" He created the plant life and said, "This is good!" After He created the animals, God again expressed, "It is good!" Then God created Adam and said, "This is *not* good!" Adam must have responded, "Who me?" What a startling thing to happen to the peak of God's creation! Here was Adam who had a good job, a good employer, good retirement benefits, nice green grass in the front lawn . . . . He had everything a man could want! Adam even had something that no person can have today—a perfect relationship with God. And God still said, "It is not good! It's not good for the man to be alone! I will make him a helpmate!" Adam was alone; he was incomplete. God then takes Adam through the process of meeting his needs of aloneness—completing him where he was incomplete. This process primarily involves building in Adam a sense of appreciation for Eve—viewing her as God's gift to him to perfectly complete him.

Within the quality of completion there are two distinct responsibilities—the husband is to be the head and the wife is to be the helpmate. Part Two, "Independence or Interdependence?" attempts to define these two most crucial functions of the marital relationship. One of the major factors behind the comparison and competition within Plan A is the gross misunderstanding of the responsibilities of head and helpmate. It's because of this misunderstanding that the man has truly trampled the woman under his feet as a doormat. Even with this "kingly," or dictatorial, position he finds an uncertainty of his identity in the house and an ache of aloneness.

The man shouldn't take all the blame. The woman normally nudges him out of the house. Now she's in charge—only to find herself overwhelmed with many pressures and left very much alone to cope with life.

A proper understanding of these responsibilities and how they interrelate offers an essential ingredient to a maximum marriage —two totally fulfilled and fully expressed individuals drawing strength from their dynamic marital oneness.

Part Three, "Battle Scars or Blessings?" moves into the area where the nitty gets gritty—communication. Love and blessing are the two foundational principles for communicating with anyone and are specifically applied to the marriage. This dynamic duo of love and blessing injected into seemingly hopeless marriages brings about positive changes toward marital oneness.

One hopeless situation was presented to me by a woman whose husband lived with another woman and would come home to her every other weekend. After explaining her tragic marriage she said, "Don't you think I have grounds for divorce?" Even though she was infuriated over her husband's actions, I sensed that she still truly loved him. So I responded, "Do you really want a divorce?" In tears she said, "What else is there to do?" Like so many people, she had run out of options. She had lost all hope of her marriage getting any better. It certainly couldn't get any worse! I explained to her the principles of love and blessing and how she might begin to apply them toward her husband the coming weekend. (It was his weekend in!) His main reason for coming home every other weekend was to accumulate things against his wife to justify his adultery. As she overwhelmed him with love and blessing that weekend, he found it difficult to mark any points against her. As a matter of fact, he actually enjoyed the weekend! He came back the following weekend just to make sure he wasn't dreaming; within three months he had moved back home permanently. At this point in time he still doesn't know what happened to him. The dynamic duo opens the door to communication!

Resting upon the foundation of love and blessing are two dimensions of communication—the spiritual and the physical. Spiritual communication is the expression of the spirit (mood or disposition) of the person behind the words being uttered. A man may come home for dinner and say, "Where's dinner?" These two words are harmless, but his spirit is the determining factor as to what is actually communicated. *Where's dinner?* could communicate *What have you been doing all day that dinner is not on the table?* Although he merely said, "Where's dinner?" he said much more! His wife hears the whole thing; so she reacts, "What do you mean what have I been doing all day?" He innocently responds, "All I said was, 'Where's dinner?'" No, that's not all he said, because he spoke with his spirit. Malachi warns us to pay attention to our spirits or we'll end up in great conflict within the marriage bond. The Book of Proverbs contains some excellent guidelines for communicating spiritually.

Physical communication is the most intimate expression of a *maximum marriage.* For too long principles and information concerning the sexual relationship have been presented outside of God's truth. The implication often is that God and sex are set against each other. On the contrary, God is for sex! Nearly every

book in the Bible has something to say about it: two books in the
Old Testament have the sexual relationship as their theme; and
the most significant illustration in the Bible of the believers' relationship to Christ is the sexual oneness of the husband-wife relationship. A verse out of the Mosaic Law sets the tone of God's
positive attitude toward physical communication:

> When a man takes a new wife, he shall not go out with the
> army, nor be charged with any duty; he shall be free at home
> one year and shall give happiness to his wife whom he has taken.
> Deuteronomy 24:5

I can't take the time to relate everything this verse is saying, but
one thing is certain—*give happiness* does not mean to tell jokes
for a year. It is clearly speaking of sexual pleasure and adjustment
for one year.

In Part Four, "Disorder or Design?" the discussion is based on
Genesis 1 and shows the purpose of God's design. Why marriage?
When one understands the *why* and the *what* of God's creation
of the marital union, then Plan B begins to fall into place. Since
God designed the family, certainly He *can* make it work!

Maximum Marriage is possible by a proper understanding and
diligent application of God's game plan for marriage—Plan B.

MAXIMUM MARRIAGE

I

Competition or Completion?

1

Wrap Her Up, I'll Take Her!

Most marriages share two common scenes: reacting to the mate's weaknesses, and placing the mate on a performance basis.

Reacting to the Mate's Weaknesses

Can you imagine this couple settling down to a nice evening at home? I can't either. Each one is caught up in a reaction against the other's weaknesses. He is tired of the burnt offerings being served for breakfast, and she complains that he's lazy. It's so natural to rebuke weaknesses and so difficult to affirm strengths.

In a Bible-study group for couples a few years ago, I tried something that I'll never try again. I opened the first meeting full of strangers saying, "Let's begin this series by sharing with us what you think is the most endearing quality about your mate." After a few moments of a threatening silence, a man stood up and said, "I haven't told my wife this, but I really appreciate her consistent loving spirit in the home. It means a lot to me." She began to well up with tears and searched for her handkerchief. Another shared, "I don't think I've ever said this to my husband, but I love his sense of stability and confidence. He gives me so much security." Her husband, moved with emotion, looked down as if to hold back from crying. One after another shared. It was a heavy time of emotion—it seemed everyone was suffering from a spring cold. The interesting thing was the words which preceded nearly everything that was shared—*I haven't told my mate but* . . . . Why do most people neglect telling strengths to their mates? It just isn't natural!

Placing the Mate on a Performance Basis

Not only is it natural to focus on the other's weaknesses, it is also easy to place the mate on the treadmill of performance. There are two lists each person carries in his frontal lobe regarding a mate—WEAKNESSES and EXPECTATIONS. For the most part these lists originated before marriage, during engagement. It was then that the man and woman began to seek counsel concerning things each would like to change in their potential mate. Each possessed a list and sought advice from various neighborhood marriage counselors—Mother, Aunt Hazel, and the like. The advice was simple and optimistic: "It'll all work out!" The couple confidently approaches the wedding day, excited about life together. Each places the list of desired changes aside assured that "It'll all work out!" After the thrill of the honeymoon wears off, each is faced with a terrible shock. Their lists were incomplete! Not only are there many *more* weaknesses that need to be changed, but the chances of changing those on the original list appear slim.

Weaknesses and expectations. Both of these scenes are characterized by *competition,* which basically consists of each mate
keeping score on what the other has done wrong and as to what
he or she is expected to do. Even the normal marital quarrels
reflect the score sheets that have been carefully recorded by each
partner.

I asked one couple who had incorporated many innovations
in quarreling (for example, throwing lamps) how a heated quar-
rel actually started. She said, "Well, it might start out by my
reminding him of . . . ." He said, "Yes, and when she brings
that up I remind her of her actions when she did . . . ." "And
when he drags that out, I remind him of the time he . . . ."
He said, "No, you don't. You tell me of the time I . . . ." She
said, "Oh, yes, that's right!" Do you see what has happened?
Each knew what the other was going to say and in the proper
order. It's as if they each have their lists of weaknesses and
expectations memorized. The only change has been the length
of the lists and the heat of the arguments. I've often wondered
why people don't tape their arguments—they're so similar. Then
each person would be freed to make faces at the other. What
an energy-saver!

Competition gnaws away at the very foundation of the marriage union. Since the world in which we live thrives on competition, it is natural to fall into this endless competitive struggle.

I found my own marriage drifting away from the oneness we
experienced at first. It was like someone was driving a wedge
between my wife and me. There was a growing distance between
us. One day I was riding along in the car with a good friend.
He was sharing some things he had learned about his own marriage. He said, "Isn't it fantastic what Genesis 2 says about
marriage?" I didn't know the first thing Genesis 2 had to say
concerning marriage. But in order to cover up my ignorance
(being a seminary graduate) I said, "Oh, that passage puts it
together all right." As soon as I could get alone I checked out
Genesis 2. It was overwhelming! I realized that I had missed the
whole purpose for my marriage.

God intended for us to function as a unit, but I had been
slicing and cutting away at Carol. I was caught up in the power

struggle! When I understood what I had done, I went home to tell Carol. I told her that I needed her, loved her, and asked her to forgive me for pushing her away through the competitive power struggle. She had experienced an "ouchy" day and didn't appear to believe my first attempt. Later I regrouped and poured out my heart to her. After that tearful experience, our marriage has never been the same.

God's idea for marriage has always involved completing one another rather than competing. Completeness was God's primary theme in the premarital counseling of Adam. He went to great lengths to bring Adam to realize how Eve was to complete him so that they could reflect the image of God in their marriage.

In order to view your mate as one who can complete you, you must commit yourself to God's process of completeness. This involves following the pattern of Adam, committing yourself to biblical principles of marriage, and enjoying the product.

Following the Pattern of Adam

Then the Lord God said, "It is not good for the man to be alone; I will make him a helper suitable for him" (Genesis 2:18). It is important to understand the background of this passage. The Lord has just finished creating everything except the peak of His creation—mankind. When God fashioned the earth, He said, "This is good!" He then created the plants and said, "This is good!" Next came the animals, and again the Lord said, "This is good!" Then the Lord created Adam and said, "This is not good!" No doubt Adam responded, "Who, me?" Imagine the shock! Adam was masterfully created with a secure vocation, outstanding working conditions, and the Creator of the universe as his employer. He even had something you and I can't have—a perfect relationship with his Creator—the God of the universe. In spite of this, God clearly declared the situation not good: "It is not good for the man to be alone" (*see* Genesis 2:18).

Alone, Adam was unable to reflect God's image, reproduce godly children, and reign in the spiritual warfare, because he was incomplete. This is why the Lord immediately followed with the resolve, "I will make him a helper suitable for him." In other words, the Lord wanted to make a helpmate who would complement Adam in order to help him reflect, reproduce, and reign. Without that helpmate Adam was alone!

In following the pattern of Adam you must realize your problem —you are alone! You cannot reflect, reproduce, and reign as God intended without your mate because God created male and female to function permanently together.

Aloneness is more than being unable to reflect, reproduce, and reign. Specifically, to the degree that your mate does not meet your needs, *you are alone!* There is the need to share emotions. Have you ever been bursting with excitement only to have your mate respond with: "That's ridiculous!" or "Don't you think before you come up with ideas like that!"? To the degree that your mate does not meet your emotional needs, *you are alone!* There is the need to stand together against trials. In most marriages the power struggle is so predominant that, instead of standing together against the trials, people normally blame each other for them. There are also spiritual and physical needs. And to the degree that your mate does not meet these needs, *you are alone.*

The awful ache of aloneness permeates every level of society, no matter the age or financial status. Let's look in on a couple filled with this pain of being alone.

"Jean and I got married three years ago when I was in my last year of engineering school; now, it seems like we always have these little picky problems that just bug me. For instance: She put me through school for a year; now she's worked two more years on top of that, so . . . she wants to have a family *right now.* She's twenty-four and I'm twenty-six, but we can't have a family right now! And the reason we can't is because I need two more years to get us situated financially before I have the responsibility of children. She cannot understand what I need to do to get us *prepared—then* we can have a family."

So this is Carl; and now, Jean, his wife of three years says, "Carl, money is not more important than our happiness, and I do not want to wait until I'm twenty-six to have a baby."

Now here is a couple having some real problems. Their marriage is not on the verge of collapse, but things are not going as well for them as they would like.

There are other complaints; he feels like she is too naggy about his clothes . . . and the trash . . . and fixing things around the apartment.

Jean says, "Well, I'm not a maid, am I? We *both* live here, and I shouldn't have to be the only one to lift a finger in the apartment and try to keep it clean. Don't forget, I've got a full-time job, too, you know."

Carl adds, "Yes . . . right . . . and that job must be making you pretty tired, especially at night, when it's time to supposedly enjoy each other's company in bed. I don't know, I try to do my part to get something going . . . but then, you're too tired. That really motivates me. It motivates me so much that I'm getting a little disinterested myself. I wish I could count the times I've thought to myself during the day, *I wish she could show some interest in trying to enjoy sex. She always waits on me to get something going. For once, I wish she could take just a little bit of initiative.*"

Although in other areas many of their needs as *persons* are being met, they both sense that something is missing and they both really want more than they're getting.

A lot of situations they handle well, but they're not *close.* They're not as close as they used to be before they got married, and they're not as close as they thought they'd be after they got married.

Jean says, "Somehow, I just feel like we don't even touch anymore. The gentleness and tenderness are just not there very often. I mean, I know we're both busy, but even when we are together and we try to talk, it just seems like there's this invisible wall there between us, bouncing our words back at us. I feel like we're together, we're in the same room, but we're not really *together—we're alone.*"

To the degree that your mate does not meet your needs *you are alone!*

In following the pattern of Adam you must acknowledge that only your mate is the perfect provision for your problem. After

God declared Adam's situation not good, He then set out to find a helpmate for Adam. He had Adam examine and name all of the animals in his search for a helpmate:

> And out of the ground the Lord God formed every beast of the field and every bird of the sky, and brought *them* to the man to see what he would call them; and whatever the man called a living creature, that was its name. And the man gave names to all the cattle, and to the birds of the sky, and to every beast of the field, but for Adam there was not found a helper suitable for him.
>
> Genesis 2:19, 20

Why did God have Adam name the animals before giving him a wife? Primarily He wanted to demonstrate to the man the nature of his incompleteness; this would also give Adam a sense of appreciation for the woman God was about to create for him. The Lord wanted Adam to realize that nothing else in the creation would be able to meet his needs of aloneness—only his mate, Eve.

Once Adam had experienced his aloneness through the naming of the animals, the Lord created the only one who could meet that need for completion—woman.

> So the Lord God caused a deep sleep to fall upon the man, and he slept; then He took one of his ribs, and closed up the flesh at that place. And the Lord God fashioned into a woman the rib which He had taken from the man, and brought her to the man.
>
> Genesis 2:21, 22

Since God created woman from one of the ribs of man, woman is part of man and therefore equal to him. It is important to note that woman is not less than man, nor was she created as an afterthought. Woman was uniquely created out of rib instead of out of the ground. She is a vital part of God's original design.

Adam had a need which God provided for through Eve. You have a need—you are alone—and God has provided for that need through your mate. You must acknowledge that your mate is God's provision for your problem of aloneness. This is not to say that you have no need for other people, but that the marital relationship is unique, completing you to a degree that no other personal relationships can.

In following the pattern of Adam you must verbalize to your mate that he or she is God's provision to complete you. When Adam awakened and saw Eve for the first time, he responded ecstatically:

> . . . "This is now bone of my bones, And flesh of my flesh; She shall be called Woman, Because she was taken out of man."
>
> Genesis 2:23

Now that hardly sounds like Adam was ecstatic! The problem is the translation of the phrase *This is now.* Have you ever gone to a football game and at an exciting moment stood up and screamed, "This is now!"? I hope not! *This is now* is not a calm expression of conversation. It's a Hebrew expletive having the force of "Wow! Wrap it up! I'll take it!" Adam went berserk! In front of God and everybody Adam went wild! He was ecstatic! It's the same kind of excitement you had when you saw the one you knew you were going to marry. Some people were so glassy-eyed they didn't know up from down.

All marriages begin with a great anticipation for the happy days ahead. The excitement of the wedding day and the thrill of the honeymoon promise the couple a happy life together. Unfortunately, after the honeymoon is over the Wow! experience often turns into *Oow!* God never intended that there should be disintegration of excitement in marriage; He designed marriage to be a dynamic and fulfilling experience, one where both man and woman are excited about one another.

So what happens? What makes the Wow! turn into *Oow!*? Remember the lists of the engagement period—the things that were going to be changed? When the "honeymoon is over," each mate comes face-to-face with the shock of his life—the list of desired changes is incomplete! Each realizes that he can't change what was on the original list let alone the newly found weaknesses! The spirit of *existence* in marriage overcomes the hope for enjoyment.

It is interesting that Adam did not react against his mate's weaknesses as many do. She certainly had a few! His response might have been, "Lord, while You're creating—she's a little chunky. Could You slim her down?" "She's too tall!" "Lord, she talks too much!" Why is it that Adam didn't respond as many do? I think the reason is that Adam was aware of something which most people ignore today. He realized that to reject Eve in any way was to reject God because God gave Eve to Adam to make him complete, to meet his aloneness needs. As Adam did, you must receive your mate as *a completer* rather than reject your mate as a competitor—an obstacle to happiness. To reject your mate in any way is to reject God and His design.

2

Throw Away Your Fig Leaves

After describing Adam's experience of receiving Eve from God, Moses breaks into the narrative and supplies principles for the process of completion.

> For this cause a man shall leave his father and his mother, and shall cleave to his wife; and they shall become one flesh.
> Genesis 2:24

Committing Yourself to Biblical Principles

Moses describes three main principles of marriage—*leave, cleave,* and *one flesh.*

Leave is the principle of severance. It's a strong word meaning to forsake or abandon. *Leaving* means to break one's dependence upon one's parents. A woman expressing to me a series of heated arguments with her husband repeatedly referred to her mother. I asked, "Does your mother live with you?" She said, "Oh, no, she lives in Fort Worth" (thirty-five miles away). "Well then, how does she get involved in these arguments?" "It's easy, I call her and she comes over." That was easy! Going back to mommy cuts away at the oneness of the relationship.

Leaving is an attitude, not necessarily a geographical change. In the patriarchal culture of the Old Testament the newly married children often lived with one set of parents. Geographically they did not go very far, but in their attitude they were to leave. A husband and wife are not to snub the parents. The way you leave is important—with parental blessing (Proverbs 1:8, 4:1). You move from an obedience relationship to an honor relationship. Dependent children should "obey your parents." Everyone ought to "honor your parents."

Cleave is the principle of permanence. It means to stick like glue. It's in the passive and should be rendered "to be cleaved by someone else." Who then does the cleaving? In Matthew 19:5, 6 it's clear that God cleaves: ". . . What therefore God has joined [cleaved] together, let no man separate." Therefore, when you commit yourself to the principle of cleaving you are committing yourself to be cleaved by God to your mate as the one who now potentially completes the image of God in your life. God's design is to mold the weaknesses and the strengths of each into a full reflection of His image. This cannot happen through competition but only through the process of completion.

Some people seem to believe that God woke up one morning and was shocked to discover that they were married the night before! God was not shocked when you were married. He is definitely involved in the business of completion. He is committed to the equation $1 + 1 = 1$ —one man plus one woman coming together forever into a beautiful oneness. Even if you feel you entered the marriage wrongly, God is still interested in working out the process of completion. Some relationships may be more difficult than others for various reasons, but that does not negate God's intent for fulfillment and full expression within the process of marital completion.

One flesh is the principle of intimacy. The oneness that results from leaving and cleaving is to be expressed free from inhibitions:

> And the man and his wife were both naked and were not ashamed.
>
> Genesis 2:25

This is not just a description of two people without clothes. The point here is that marriage is to be a close, uninhibited oneness even to the most intimate relationship—the physical. Total communication!

Enjoying the Product

The results of committing yourself to the process of completion rather than competition are significant. First of all you are freed from reacting to your mate's weaknesses.

You don't have to be married long to get the picture that you are linked up with a real *person* who comes complete with a first-class set of weaknesses. During the days of courtship they are unnoticed; during the early days of marriage they are overlooked; now, however, they are getting to be unbearable.

You know it's one thing when he watches three football games on the two-day honeymoon, but now out of a total of twenty-three hours of football on the tube over Thanksgiving he watches twenty-one hours. The other two hours he fell asleep on the sofa.

I'm thinking of a wife who began to sense growing irritation and frustration because of weaknesses and faults in her husband. As an example of the situation they were involved in, it might be interesting to just relive a typical day. Many wives will identify with this.

In the morning she gets up first to feed the children, while he catches an extra thirty minutes in the sack. So, right off the bat she resents him for being lazy. Under her breath she's saying to herself, "It's always *Daddy* when company is here, and *Mommy* when it's time for breakfast."

Finally, when he does fall out of bed, he makes a mad dash for his bath, scans the sports page while hastily eating breakfast, and then flashes by her as he jumps into his car and speeds off down the freeway to work.

Meanwhile, her problems have only just begun as she picks up the trail he has left behind him on his journey from the bed to the front door. Socks, underwear, wet towels, newspapers, and bathrobe clearly mark his path.

Once the path has been cleared, she is faced with overhauling the bathroom. First of all, she picks the soap out of the tub water where he has left it to get soft; then she drains and cleans the tub and hangs up his towel and washcloth. Then not only is there water all over the side of the sink and floor where he has been shaving, but it's all over the mirror and walls. So she wipes all that off and puts away his razor, deodorant, toothbrush, toothpaste, comb, hairspray, and finally unplugs his hot lather machine.

Meanwhile, the children have completely demolished the living room, the day is half over, and she's beginning to realize that this guy she thought was her real heartthrob is turning out to be a royal pain in the neck.

The day progresses; he's forty-five minutes late for dinner, comes home and gobbles down the dinner she's worked three hours on, then props himself on the sofa to yuk it up with Dandy Don and the rest of the boys on Monday-night football. Meanwhile she's bathing and dressing the kids for bed, straightening up the house, and getting ready for her little stretch with Monday night at the dishes. After all, what are women for? He takes care of the office, she takes care of the house.

Application of the principle? The day this woman committed herself to God's principle of completeness is the day she began to see God turn these weak areas of her husband's life into opportunities of blessing for her. And, ladies, if God can bless you through football, then there is no limit to how you can be blessed.

When you realize God's design is to bring about a oneness between man and woman (even through their weaknesses), you are released from the normal cutting response against your mate. You must view your mate's weaknesses for what they actually are—tools in the hands of God to fashion your marriage into a more complete reflection of His image.

As you accept God's design your mate is released from the feeling of being evaluated by performance. It's only as you view your mate as God's perfect gift to complete you that you are able to take him or her off the performance treadmill. You no longer treat your mate as a competitor. When a mate feels totally accepted, that very atmosphere of acceptance and excitement encourages greater performance than ever.

The treadmill experience encourages a sense of inadequacy. My wife and I traveled throughout the country during our college years ministering in churches. We noticed with interest the different pastors and their wives since we were moving in that direction ourselves. Much to our surprise we found that every pastor's wife played the piano. This began to eat away at Carol, because she didn't play the piano. Out of her frustration she began to tell me how I was getting a bad deal, since she couldn't play the piano. After repeated outbursts like this, I quietly began to agree. We carried this wonderful little treadmill into our marriage. When the honeymoon was over, her sense of inadequacy surfaced in other areas. Naturally I was very helpful in encouraging her depression through my quiet agreement. This ridiculous cycle continued until I realized what the principle of completeness was all about. The sense of inadequacy has vanished!

A commitment to completeness will affect a change in your mate without nagging. One couple, whose marriage was filled with explosive "discussions," came to me seeking help. Their arguments normally climaxed in throwing things. He didn't seem too open, so I sent him into another room. I asked her, "When did all of this start?" She said, "Three months ago I realized that he rarely came home on time, so I set up a rule." I knew this was going to be a winner! When I inquired about the rule, she rose to the occasion with a new one. "I told him that if he didn't come home at five-thirty he couldn't eat!" What happened? He hadn't come home at that time for the three months. I asked, "Would you say on the basis of the three-month experience that your rule is working?" She nervously laughed and said, "I never thought of it that way!"

This couple was competing by keeping score. She was saying, "I have the right for you to be home at a decent time in the evening!" That made the score 1–0. Not wanting to win, but just to keep the score even, he began to say, "Well, I have the right to stay out as late as I wish—and even eat better!" 1–1!

I explained the concept of completeness to her. The logical application of the principle was for her to revoke the rule. I suggested that she tell him that he could come home any time he wanted and she would feed him the best. That was a lot for her to grasp! But she did! In the next two weeks her husband came home at five-thirty on the dot. On one day, after realizing that I had a definite part in her actions, he called me at exactly five-thirty and said, "I'm home!" and hung up. This wife saw a significant change in her husband's behavior through a commitment to completeness.

Suggested Steps to Completeness

Notice that these are suggested steps. The Bible doesn't present many steps. It presents principles which are absolute. The application of the absolute principles may vary from person to person and from situation to situation. So you may take the following steps and throw them out, burn them, or you may even embrace them as your own. But whatever you do, you must seek to apply the principle of completeness!

Your mate's weaknesses (or apparent weaknesses) are God's tools for developing you as a couple who can fully express His image. When you label something as a weakness, it is a value judgment on your part. It may not really be a weakness at all. But, regardless, God is concerned primarily about your response. James says: "Consider it all joy, my brethren, when you encounter various trials, knowing that the testing of your faith produces endurance" (1:2, 3). I'd like to find out who caused the "various trials" so I could get them. James doesn't give us a clue to the cause, but is very clear as to what our response should be. In the Sermon on the Mount, Jesus relates an illustration of the phantom hand coming out of nowhere and slapping you on the cheek. I would want to know, *Who hit me?* Jesus ignores that. He wants to know what I will do with the other side of my face. We are to respond properly. He will deal with the offender.

Step 1   Alone, without your mate being present, list in one column your mate's STRENGTHS and in another column WEAKNESSES. Then list your WRONG RESPONSES. It's so easy to point a finger at your mate and so difficult to admit any personal wrongs. Jesus speaks to this:

> And why do you look at the speck in your brother's [mate's] eye, but do not notice the log that is in your own eye? Or how can you say to your brother [mate], "Let me take the speck out of your eye," and behold, the log is in your own eye? You hypocrite, first take the log out of your own eye, and then you will see clearly *enough* to take the speck out of your brother's [mate's] eye.
>
> Matthew 7:3–5

Satan says, "Look at that weakness. Can you believe he loves you and still does that? Get him!"

God says, "Don't look at that weakness. Look at Me and respond properly. I'll work on the weakness!"

After listening and evaluating what one couple's problems were, I determined that I needed to take Jane, the wife, through the steps to completeness with her husband, Bob. I started with the question, "What are your husband's strengths?"

"He doesn't have any!"

"Lady, you must have had something that drew you to him when you married!"

She responded, "That's why I'm here! I can't figure out *why* I married him!"

Since I get paid for filling up columns, I pressed on to get her to list Bob's strengths; I probed and probed. Finally I hit on something as I asked, "Does he give you any money?" She threw out an amount that was more than I was making at the time. Excitedly I said, "Alright, there's a strength—money!" A list is hardly one item, so I continued the search; I asked if she had her own car.

She chuckled and said, "Bob gave me a new Eldorado for my birthday two months ago!"

"An Eldorado—that's a strength!" Well, we didn't have much, but at least we had the start of a list.

When I asked about Bob's weaknesses, she lit up. That's what she came to discuss. The first weakness she mentioned was *food!* She said, "All he does is eat, eat, eat! He's 272 pounds and growing!" The second weakness she listed: "He doesn't pay attention to me. When he comes home in the evening he walks right to the phone. He doesn't even acknowledge I exist!" The third of her husband's weaknesses was interesting. She said, "Now my husband is a Christian, but sometimes he gets so ticked-off he cusses me out!"

She had many more weaknesses to share with me, but I encouraged her to move on to the next column—WRONG RESPONSES. I asked, "What do you do wrong when your husband does these things?" She appeared puzzled and said, "Huh?" She had no capacity to understand that she was doing anything wrong in response to his weaknesses. Realizing that I was getting absolutely nowhere, I shifted gears and said, "Well, what do you do when he does these horrible things?" She told me that when her husband ate too much, she had a real gift for cutting him down verbally. At an executive party where Bob wanted to impress his boss Jane really took a "shot" at him. Bob was at the chip-and-dip table across the den. Jane yelled, "Bounce over here, Bob!" (Naturally, that's not the kind of encouragement that enhances a relationship.)

I asked, "What do you do when he doesn't pay attention to you?"

"I don't pay attention to him!"

"And if he cusses you out?"

"I cuss him right back!"

When I was going through this chart on my own marriage, I discovered some interesting things. After filling out the strengths column, I moved to the column for weaknesses. Only one weakness kept staring me in the face—my wife is slow! I mean SLOW!! (In Francis Schaeffer terminology she is *slow slow.*)

If we would be going to someone's home for dinner (to bless their lives), the normal scene could be described as hectic. I get ready (thinking what to expect throughout the evening). As the time for departure draws nigh I stand near the front door and yell back in a melodious voice, "Are you ready?" When Carol appears in the hallway, it just takes a quick glance to realize that if she is ready we're both in a heap of trouble! So she goes back to the bedroom to continue making herself ready for the evening. As it gets later and later my "spiritual gift" for sarcasm and cutting remarks surfaces. If we're going to dinner, I'll say, "Honey, let me call them and tell them we'll make it for dessert, okay?" Through this little jab I manage to arouse a reaction from her. The verbal sparring builds toward an incredible silent, yet intense, atmosphere in the car. All that can be heard during the entire twenty-minute ride to the dinner is a periodic, exasperated sigh! This sigh is an offensive device warning the other that you're still steaming. When we arrive at our destination thirty minutes late, we must act as if nothing has happened. I open the door for Carol and we both paste on the plastic smile, but still remain silent. When we are greeted at the door by our host he says, "How are you?" "Oh, fine. Couldn't be better!" we both agree.

Step 2   Confess to God your wrong responses.

In order to demonstrate clearly to Jane that her responses to Bob's weaknesses were wrong, I wrote SIN over the column. The long list now needed to be acknowledged as wrong on her part.

I thought she understood, so we began to pray. I prayed a little, and she prayed a little. (She prayed about her missionary sister in Africa.) Then I prayed she would have the courage to confess them. After a nice season of prayer, I said, "Hold it! We are praying so that you can confess these wrong responses against your husband!" It was like trying to land an airplane, but we couldn't. We just kept circling the field. Finally, she landed that airplane—she confessed her wrong responses to God. It was at this point that she realized that *at least* half of their problem stemmed from her actions. She was truly broken over it!

Step 3   Thank God for your partner and especially for those areas you don't like.

I read 1 Thessalonians 5:18 to Jane: "in everything give thanks; for this is God's will for you in Christ Jesus." It doesn't say we should be running around trying to be filled with thankfulness when someone hurts us. Paul is not commanding a feeling—be thankful—but an act of the will—"give thanks." Give thanks in everything, even when you don't feel like it. Why? Because God will take even the adverse things that interrupt our lives and work them together with something else for our good (*see* Romans 8:28).

Jane asked, "You mean I must give thanks for Bob's excessive eating?" "Yes, and worse than that, his temper, and his lack of paying attention to you!" We took off in our airplane again and seemed to circle the field much longer than before (praying around the world). However, it was worth all of the "flying time," when I heard her genuinely thank God for her husband and specifically for his weaknesses. The fog was clearing in her mind so that she could see Bob as her completer not as her competitor.

Step 4   Ask, "How does God want to use that weakness as a positive tool to bring my marriage to a more complete reflection of His image? What is it that God wants to teach me through my mate's weaknesses?"

This is the question I asked concerning my wife's classic weakness of being *slow!* My first answer was *Patience!* Although I could use an additional amount of patience, I felt it was a cop-out. Then I decided to ask my wife.

So I asked her, "Honey, what can I do to help *us* get ready on time?" Now, I didn't really mean that. I really meant *What can I do to help you get over your problem of being so slow?* But I said it properly, "What can I do to help *us* get ready on time?"

"Well, the first thing . . ." she began.

That scared me! *First* implied very strongly that there may be a *second* or even a *third* to follow. It was as if someone had prepared her for my question. She had a list!!

She said, "The first thing, you could hang up your clothes. Then, you could help get the children ready for bed."

"You do that too, huh? Okay! I'll hang up my clothes and help with the children."

"Finally," she continued, "maybe you could get ready early and troubleshoot around the house when someone calls or comes to the door. Instead of yelling from the bathroom, 'Honey, would you get that?' maybe you could get it."

The entire dialogue sent me into a state of shock! It was as if I had walked into the bedroom with a twenty-gauge shotgun aimed directly at my wife's weakness—*slow slow!*—and right when I pulled the trigger, my gun blew up on me! What I thought was *her* problem turned out to be all *mine!* God was not trying to teach me *patience,* but *sensitivity* to my wife's needs!

Step 5   Write out a commitment to completeness to your mate and read it out loud to your mate.

Three items should be included in this written commitment. First, there must be a confession, without condemnation. This might be a confession of rejecting your mate in various areas or of your wrong responses. Notice I said *confession without condemnation.* Confession with condemnation is, "Honey, I'm so sorry I acted that way last night . . . but you *know* how much I dislike that!" It is to be without any condemnation!

Second, there needs to be a resolve on your part to look beyond your mate's weaknesses to God. Don't focus on the weaknesses! Allow God to mold your marriage into a better reflection of His image through them!

Third, you must thank God for your mate—God's gift to you to perfectly complete you.

These three items may not say all you want to say. Don't be bound by them. The important thrust of Step 5 is *verbalization.* I wouldn't suggest, "Bone of my bones, and flesh of my flesh."

You may stir up a violent reaction. "Wow!" even loses its effect after a while! You'll think of something.

Bob came in to see me a few days after my session with Jane. He was so nervous! From the moment he walked in I sensed he wanted to tell me something. But each time I inquired he stammered and stuttered and mumbled the conversation into oblivion. Finally, I was able to pin him down and help him blurt it out.

He said, "Do you know what my wife did yesterday? She walked over to me, kissed me, and said, 'Bob, I love you and I need you.' She *really* meant it!"

I asked, "What did you say?"

In an embarrassed sort of way he said, "I told her, 'I need you, too!'"

That's what completion is all about! It's not merely accepting your mate as he or she is. It's more than that! It's actually receiving your mate as a gift from God to perfectly complete you, knowing that to reject your mate in any way, shape, or form is to reject God and His design for oneness.

Competition? No! Completion!

II

Independence or Interdependence?

3

"I. M. De Head"

In heaven all the men were separated from their wives and were asked to fall into line behind one of two signs. The sign on the left read HENPECKED HUSBANDS. The sign over on the right said THE HEADS! It was an incredible sight! Every husband fell into line behind the sign HENPECKED HUSBANDS. Everyone, that is, except one little man. This one man, out of all husbands ever, was standing conspicuously alone behind the sign THE HEADS. A reporter covering the event rushed over to interview this unique man. He said, "Sir, this is unbelievable! Here you are, out of all these men, standing in the line designated for husbands who have been the heads of their homes. How is it that you were able to walk into this line as the only head *ever* on earth?" The man said, "Well, I don't know. My wife just told me to stand here!"

So much of the marital humor in this century reflects the gross misunderstanding of *headship* in the home. One of the greatest tragedies today is the loss of a clear comprehension of headship. Because of the poverty of understanding and its disastrous effects, I guess people would rather laugh than cry about it. It is no joke! This misunderstanding of headship is hurling a crushing blow to the identity of male and female, to the security of the children, and to the very foundation of the social structure of the home. As the basic sociological unit of the home is shattered, so the entire society begins to fragment and disintegrate.

Christian seminars and literature are saturated with material for the woman's role without adequate consideration of the man as head of the home. To beat the women over the head with submission without a proper perspective on headship muddies the water. The result—misconceptions flow. Non-Christian wives are confounded by the master-slave image, which is not true; Christian wives are ignorantly submitting, suffering from a "holy" misery, which should not be; and the husbands continue to nonchalantly ignore their responsibility in the home, which is intolerable!

Misconceptions of Headship

"Mr. Dick Tater"

One misconception is to think of the head of the home as a dictator. He is not a person who gives all of the orders in a dictatorial style, expecting every breath to arouse an immediate response. Some think of the head as one who must snap a bull-whip with constant demands—the master-slave relationship. This is completely wrong!

"Mr. Waterwalker"

Another misconception many have is that a man must be nearly perfect (know more Bible verses than his wife) to be the head. We must get one thing straight right now! The man was not chosen as head because he has everything going for him or because he is outstanding. No matter how inadequate a man feels, or actually is, does not change the fact that the man is to be the head.

"Mr. I. M. DeHead"

Still another misconception of headship is to think that merely announcing oneself as head is sufficient. After being motivated to be the heads of their homes, many men go home and announce, "I am the head!" His wife doesn't believe him; no one else votes for him. So the man retreats. He may hear a speaker talk on the subject or read a book which recharges his motivation. So he goes home and tries it again—this time with a little hesitation. "I am the head! Okay? Can I be? Maybe—just tonight?" This cycle continues. It only varies in degrees until the man gives up.

He is substituting the proclamation of headship for the function of it. Some men continue to express the idea that the man is to be head and the woman is to submit in order to convince themselves of their own responsibility. The lack of the confidence of others in the house, together with the lack of knowledge of his responsibility, force the man to announce himself as head rather than act like it.

Meaning of Headship

Just what is a *spiritual head? Headship* includes two dimensions—God's representative authority and sacrificial lover. It's interesting that the man is not explicitly told to be the head of his wife. But the wife is clearly instructed to be submissive to her husband as head. The husband is to be the head over the wife, but his function is not to "lord it" over her. He's not to be the army sergeant shouting orders. He is set up as representative authority in the home. That's his position! His function is to be sacrificial lover! (This balance will be extensively illustrated in the discussion of the Model of Headship.)

As God's representative authority in the marital relationship you are in charge of all the responsibilities in the home. You are set up as authority over your wife and children.

Authority does not mean "better than." Pure authority is much different! A good illustration of pure authority in operation is a traffic cop. When he or she blows the whistle or motions for you to stop, you stop! Why? Not because the traffic cop is better than you, but because of the authority given one who wears a police badge. So you submit to the authority. Even within the biblical explanation of the Trinity you find authority in operation. God the Father is head over God the Son, yet they are equal and one. Pure authority does not negate equality.

Authority was established in all relationships of life for at least three reasons: (1) No one can assume all responsibilities. Each head needs a helpmate for support in order to accomplish what needs to be done. Each helpmate needs a head as a "shock absorber" against the pressures of all responsibility. (2) Waywardness is suppressed by the orderliness of a line of authority. Chaos reigns otherwise! (3) It enables human relationships to function more smoothly. In every relationship—such as home, committee, business, government—someone must be in charge, or accountable, in order to promote ease in decision making.

To be a representative authority is not only to be in charge of your home; you are held responsible for your wife and children. That's a sobering responsibility!

As sacrificial lover you are to give of yourself totally. You are responsible to be the servant of your wife—to be actively seeking to meet her needs. You might give up a golf game or tennis match just to do something special with your wife. It's not to be done when convenient, but always—sacrificially! Is there a woman in the world who would refuse to respond positively when treated with sacrificial love?

When headship is properly understood and in operation the man and wife discover a new freedom. The husband is freed from self-centeredness and the wife is freed from subjugation through the sacrificial love of headship.

Model of Headship

Jesus is the ideal man, and His function as head is illustrated best by His relationship with His disciples. Let's look at a few illustrations of headship in the life of Jesus which serve specifically as models for the man.

First, Jesus was in total submission to the Father. In the same way the husband should be a man in submission to God: "I urge you therefore, brethren, by the mercies of God, to present your bodies a living and holy sacrifice, acceptable to God, which is your spiritual service of worship" (Romans 12:1). You, as a husband, must submit yourself to God as the Designer of the family. However, submission extends further than directly to God. Submission to God is demonstrated through submission in other areas. There is to be submission to the government (*see* 1 Peter 2:13), to your employer (*see* v. 18), and to other believers (*see* Ephesians 5:21). The latter includes your wife! All of these areas of submission are to be "in the fear of God."

Your submission to God is the best example your wife has to observe. Any lack of submission on her part may have been learned from your lack of submission. She may have picked up your bad attitudes concerning your employer or your bending of certain laws of the government—traffic violations, income-tax evasions, and the like.

Your submission to God will give your wife a deep sense of security. Can you imagine committing your entire welfare into the hands of another person? That could be an uneasy arrangement! You as a human are suspect and fickle. God is stable and absolute. Knowing that you are dependent upon God and look to Him for your direction in life should release her from fear in accepting and responding to your headship.

Submission is the key to your own self-image as head. Jesus repeated a principle throughout His ministry that is directly contrary to man's normal attitude. For a man to find himself, he must lose himself. For a man to live, he must die. This principle is uniquely applicable to the husband's desire to function properly as spiritual head. For you to function maximally as head you must die to yourself by total submission to God. When you die to yourself and self-centered interests, your wife is motivated to trust fully in you as the head. That gives you a sense of real confidence in being the spiritual head and encourages you to die to yourself in submission to God in other areas. And the cycle continues.

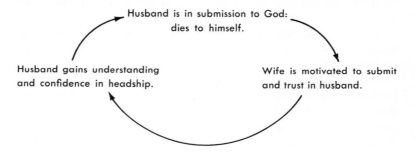

Husband is in submission to God: dies to himself.

Husband gains understanding and confidence in headship.

Wife is motivated to submit and trust in husband.

Second, as a model of headship, Jesus showed His men that He loved them: "Greater love has no one than this, that one lay down his life for his friends" (John 15:13). The husband should seek to love his wife in the same way—giving himself up for his wife. This love doesn't have to manifest itself through outstanding actions. Too many men fail to realize that little things communicate love in a powerfully expressive way. I take my wife out to a nice dinner quite often. However, many times after an expensive evening out, my wife will respond, "I really enjoyed the evening, but I feel stuffed!" In other words, I just spent a lot of money to make my wife feel uncomfortable. I have learned through many similar evenings that the big demonstrations of love are not necessarily the most meaningful. When I arrive home with a bunch of flowers which cost very little, my wife is ecstatic! Little expressions of love communicate so effectively. (They are even a better investment!)

Sacrificial love is redemptive. It redeems you from selfishness because you are caught up in giving and giving to another, rather than thinking of yourself. When I was assistant pastor, I had many "training" experiences. *Training* is the name given to the performing of responsibilities that are located far down the pastor's priority list. One area of "training" was to be present in the fathers' waiting room of the maternity ward. Now there is nothing more ugly than somebody else's baby! It doesn't take many experiences with ecstatic fathers to learn new ways to express your excitement without lying about it. You find yourself saying things like, "My, that sure is a baby, isn't it?" Because of the hysterical atmosphere they don't even hear you. They have gone berserk with camera and flashcubes in hand! They make comments like, "She knows me!" (The babies can't even focus their eyes for sixteen weeks!) I determined that I would never act like that.

When Tammy was about to be born, Carol convinced me that I should take my camera for a few pictures. As I waited in the fathers' room I couldn't believe the behavior of some of those men. Then when my name was called, something came over me— it was the same kind of possession! I went berserk, just like all the rest! I couldn't control myself! Tammy was the most beautiful baby I had ever seen in my life! In the first twenty-four hours I took fifty-six slides! (I'm sure she thought her dad had a camera for a nose!) I even think she recognized me! Then when I was permitted to hold her in my arms, I realized that there was a love oozing out of me that I didn't know I had.

When our second daughter, Tacy, was born, I thought I had learned how to contain myself. But it happened all over again!

I now live with three women, my wife, Tammy, and Tacy. I'm "hooked" on loving them sacrificially, so that all I do and think concerning them is how to give and give. That takes up so much of my time that I have very little left for me! That's good! Sacrificial love redeems you from selfishness.

Third, Jesus as the leader demonstrated profound understanding. For instance, He knew that the adulterous woman needed forgiveness and not rebuke (*see* John 8:10, 11). Similarly, the husband should give his wife the feeling that he understands her deepest needs. "You husbands likewise, live with your wives in an understanding way . . ." (1 Peter 3:7). The phrase "live with your wives" is only used here in the New Testament. It is used several times in the Old Testament with the idea of sexual union in marriage. Peter seems to be saying here to live with your wife in such a way as to meet her needs—even to the most intimate needs of sex. To live with your wife "in an understanding way" is to become an active student of your wife. It is to have investigative insight into what makes her tick or ticked-off. (That's an important difference to know!)

In addition to this, your wife needs to sense that you are on her team—to know that you are interested in and understand her every frustration and concern.

When Carol and I were involved in the campus ministry, I learned this principle firsthand. We were ministering on a campus with a 70 percent Jewish population. From the beginning we had an excellent relationship with the campus rabbi. He was very warm to us and even defended us in a few critical situations. One day he expressed a desire to talk with us about our views of the Messiah. We set up an appointment with him for a later date. It was an exciting open door for us to discuss the Messianic claims of Jesus. On the day of the appointment Carol had taken Tammy (five months old) in to her pediatrician. About twenty minutes before seeing the rabbi I got the word to call Carol. I called and all I heard was crying on the other end. As she began to make sense I realized what had happened. Tammy was going to have to wear a hip brace for six months. Carol was crushed. (Now most of the experiences I share are my mistakes, but this time I did the right thing.) I could have said a lot of things like, "Honey, what do you think her life expectancy is, seventy years? What's six months out of seventy years?" But instead of ridiculing her concern, I jumped on her team. I said, "Honey, do you want me to come home?" Her entire expression changed immediately, "But you've got to see the rabbi. No! I'm alright! Everything's fine!" What happened? She only needed the supportive feeling of her husband being on her team.

Fourth, Jesus taught them how to believe God. He constantly moved from lecture to life (*see* Mark 9:35–41). The husband should structure an atmosphere in the home of believing God in all things. No matter who knows the most about the Bible, you must set the pace spiritually in the home. This is not to say that your wife should never initiate anything spiritual, but that you need to take the responsibility for creating an atmosphere of turning to God whether in times of crisis or in the normal business of life. There undoubtedly will be times when your wife will approach you with, "Honey, can't we pray?" That definitely sounds like, "Oh, atheist husband of mine, don't you believe in prayer anymore?" Although it isn't the most tactful way of approaching you, she is still attempting to communicate to you a real need. She wants to pray together!

The month after Tammy was born Carol was in the process of gathering up borrowed maternity clothes and returning them. One morning, while searching desperately for a scarf which belonged to a certain dress, our happy time turned into a frantic chaos of screams and tears. I was following Carol around asking her helpful questions like, "Well, where did you have it last?" (Obviously if she had known that, she would have gone and picked it up!) Out of complete desperation I stopped Carol in the hall, put my arm around her, and said, "Honey, we are going to pray! Not that *God* will find that silly scarf, but that He'll calm us down so that *we* can find it!" I prayed and went on to work. Carol found the scarf that afternoon. At the end of the year we had a final meeting with the students and staff involved in the ministry. We were sharing the highlights of the year in each of our lives. The sharing progressed around the circle to Carol. Can you imagine what she shared? Right! That dumb scarf episode. I had forgotten about it! But it was a significant event in her year. Even the most insignificant actions help to create an atmosphere of believing God.

Fifth, Jesus accepted total responsibility for the men who trusted their lives to Him (*see* Mark 10:45). Similarly, the husband should accept total responsibility for his wife. The husband has the responsibility for "taking care of his own household" (*see* 1 Timothy 3:4, 5). As much as I hate to admit it, when my wife is experiencing frustration or a particular problem, it normally relates directly back to my irresponsibility in some area. This proves to be true in nearly every marital counseling situation in which I have participated. If your wife has a problem, check out your contribution to it. It's usually considerable!

When I was writing my first book, I allowed myself to be placed under an impossible deadline. During the last two weeks I literally worked night and day. It was a family project! I worked in a small ten-by-twelve-foot room in our apartment. Every hour or so I staggered out of the room to read my "bestseller" to Carol. Carol's job was to respond with encouraging *oohs* and *ahs* and make me another glass of iced tea. I noticed on about the ninth or tenth day that her *oohs* and *ahs* were getting weaker. (As a matter of fact, so was the tea!) The way she handed me the glass of tea communicated clearly. Her disposition said, *Hope you choke on an ice cube!* I knew I was in trouble, but I had to make my deadline! That evening, as I paused from typing to think, I heard Carol sobbing in the bedroom. I knew what the problem was. I had not given anything to our relationship. Now I was receiving the results—weak tea and tears! I went in, sat down next to her, and said, "I know what the problem is." From her sobs she muttered, "You do?" "Yes, it's me! I haven't been contributing positively to our marriage and you're paying for it." This triggered a flood of tears that seemed to say *I agree!*

Sixth, Jesus solved the problems that His men brought to Him (*see* Mark 1:30, 31; 8:4). The husband should take on every problem his wife brings to him and search for solutions (*see* 1 Timothy 3:4, 5). It's so easy to say, "That's your problem! You dug the hole. Let me help you into it!" *Taking care of your wife* means that her problem becomes your problem. Not to take on your wife's problems when they arise is just to put them off until later.

A very tense time in our marriage occurs when I inspect Carol's checkbook. Generally, she forgets to record the details of her check writing, like what she wrote it for and where she wrote it. (Some people are paid to do nothing but keep a record of one's check writing. They are called *banks!* Each month they send you a letter with a notice of how much money you lack in your checking account. It's quite embarrassing!) There have been times when I've opened her checkbook and found two full pages blank—with no record to back them up! Now there are a lot of ways to handle this predicament. You could pat her on the back and sympathetically express, "When they come and get you, I'll take care of the kids and pray for you." That is an option, but it is not the way to function as head. In this situation you must jump in there and start subtracting. It can't be "that's your problem," but "that's our problem."

Mandate for Headship

The two commands found in Ephesians are strong challenges to the spiritual head:

> Husbands, love your wives, just as Christ also loved the church and gave Himself up for her; that He might sanctify her, having cleansed her by the washing of water with the word, that He might present to Himself the church in all her glory, having no spot or wrinkle or any such thing; but that she should be holy and blameless. So husbands ought also to love their own wives as their own bodies. He who loves his own wife loves himself; for no one ever hated his own flesh, but nourishes and cherishes it, just as Christ also does the church, because we are members of His body.
>
> Ephesians 5:25–30

In this passage Paul illustrates what the husband-wife relationship should be—by the relationship of Christ and the church. Everything mentioned about Christ and the church is true of the husband-wife relationship, except one—Jesus is the Saviour of the body, the husband is not.

The first command is to love your wife as Christ loved the church and gave Himself up for her. This is the sacrificial love mentioned earlier. Your sacrificial love for your wife is to accomplish two things. First, it should "sanctify her." Your love is to set your wife apart from other women as someone special. Second, your sacrificial love is to elevate your wife to be a glorious woman without "spot or wrinkle or any such thing." Your love should be lifting your wife up and motivating her toward being a glorious, beautiful woman. That's appealing! But more than this, she will be pleasing to God by being "holy and blameless." That's what your sacrificial love is to do for your wife! Is it working?

The second command is to love your wife as your own body. This doesn't mean to love your wife as much as you love your own body, but to love her as your own body, because she is one with you. Paul uses two words to describe this kind of love— *nourish* and *cherish. Nourish* means to build up or give strength to. (Not cutting down or slicing away.) *Cherish* has the meaning of tenderly caring for, with special emphasis on warmth and tenderness. You wouldn't sling your wife onto the couch and roughly say, "Sit down, I'm going to kiss you!" Women just don't respond to that! They respond to tenderness and warmth (we'll see this more specifically in chapter 8, "Where's Dinner?").

Suggested Steps of Action

Step 1 *Confess any rebellion against those above you in authority and resolve to submit to them.* From your perspective it's unreasonable to expect your wife to follow the line of authority when you are unwilling to do so. Remember you are the best example your wife and family have to observe concerning authority.

Step 2 *Together with your wife, make a list of every responsibility she is presently assuming in the house.* Be prepared for a shock! One couple listed sixty-six things the wife is responsible for doing each week!

I think it's important to note that a woman can conceivably assume any responsibility in the home from scrubbing floors to handling the finances. But the husband is still head in each of the areas. He is still held responsible over the wife no matter the responsibility.

Step 3 *Agree to assume certain responsibilities:* those she presently does not feel competent enough to perform without extreme tension, or those which cause her extreme frustration. This will vary with ages and size of the family. In both instances you are trying to eliminate that which causes excessive pressure. It's this kind of pressure that is the root cause of much of the tightness and lack of responsiveness in many women today. Resentment follows on the heels of this pressure causing women to get out of the home at all cost (even divorce). You as the head must alleviate this pressure. That's your job as a shock absorber! Let me illustrate a couple of pressurized scenes in most homes.

When we were in a campus ministry, we were supported by churches and friends on a monthly basis. We were paid on the twelfth of the month. Each month, during the first twelve days,

I would begin to think that we might have a short check that
month. (Over the four-year period we only received one short
check.) I didn't realize the pressure I was placing upon Carol
until she asked some revealing questions. She would say things
like, "When they take our car, do we actually drive it to the
bank, or do they come after it?" She also bought a book on
101 ways to fix beans. It didn't take many of these hints to wake
me up to the extreme pressure she was experiencing through
finances. So I relieved the pressure by setting up a household
account and shutting my mouth about financial concerns. (Especially unfounded ones!) The household account includes every
need Carol has in order to function in her responsibilities (food,
clothes, baby-sitting, etc.). This comes out of our paycheck first.
If we come up short, I need to absorb most of the pressure. This
method has really worked! Carol thinks we're wealthy! She's
budgeting, giving, and cutting corners—we don't eat much any
more!—but the pressure is off my wife so that she can joyfully
respond to me and fulfill her responsibilities in life.

Though financial pressure is a common problem in marriages
today, there is a universal problem which the head can help to
solve. For a woman with young children the most frenzied time
of day (of her life, for that matter!) is from around five o'clock
to when the children are in bed. This is when she must juggle
the children—spilled milk, sibling rivalries, a barrage of questions
—and fix dinner at the same time. It's affectionately known as
the "pit." Some women call it the "valley of the shadow." About
the time everything is unglued, "the king" arrives home. He usually moves toward his throne where he reads his paper and yells
little tidbits of encouragement into the kitchen. "What's for dinner tonight?" "Meatloaf." "Oooh," he says in a disappointed tone.
When the dinner is ready the commotion reaches a climax with
numerous yells: "Let's eat!" "Come to the table—right now! I said,
'right now!'" There is a final, "Let's pray." (That almost seems
out of place here!)

After dinner "the king" moves to his second throne—sitting
before the big electric tube. Here he watches Agent 002 and
observes how suave and cool that operator is. "The king" progres-
sively begins to identify with Agent 002 thinking, *I'm as suave*

and cool as Agent 002! He's getting more and more psyched up about how swift he really is. Meanwhile, his wife is bathing the children, washing the dishes, cleaning up the kitchen, and putting the kids to bed. (This includes the second and third drinks of water, several dry potty-runs, and chasing the tigers out of each bedroom.) Then she makes one last picking-up tour of the house and heads toward the bedroom suite. She finally staggers into the bedroom about ten o'clock. "The king" (who by now is really Agent 002) says seductively, "Hey, love, how about tonight?" She mumbles back, "How about *what* tonight?"

If you want to assume the responsibility of headship, you must function during the "valley of the shadow." Who says you "punch out" at 5:30 P.M. or 6:00 P.M.? Your wife doesn't! *So why should you?* You must move in there and help.

Fortunately, when I arrive home my wife doesn't want me to cook. So I must help with the children—removing them from the kitchen. For the longest time, I had to come home and *wing* with my two children. (That's *swing*—for those who are uninitiated.) I got so tired of "winging," but it made dinner a whole lot better!

After dinner, it's my job to clear the table while Carol puts the children in the tub. Then while Carol fills the dishwasher and cleans up the kitchen, I'm getting the kids out of the tub and dressed for bed. When I function as head during the "valley of the shadow," we're able to cut the time required by over an hour. Now we can stagger into the bedroom *together* and enjoy one another.

Step 4 *Separately, fill out a need-sheet, making three columns.* On one side list your emotional, spiritual, and physical needs. On the other side list your mate's emotional, spiritual, and physical needs. Exchange papers and discuss them. No matter how you discover her needs, do it!

Step 5 *Implement a personalized program to meet her needs.* Don't get caught announcing yourself as "I. M. De Head" without acting like it!

Will you commit yourself to the responsibility of headship—God's representative authority and sacrificial lover?

4

So Who Wants To Be a Doormat?

Doormats are for wiping the dirt off your shoes. *So who wants to be a doormat?*

Misunderstanding in the area of submission has caused a great deal of emotional reaction. The most vocal of these reactions is the women's-liberation movement. The leaders of this movement have been effectively exposing a real problem—the subjugation and exploitation of women. The woman is the doormat of the world! For the most part I agree with their evaluation of the problems women face in our world. Because of the confusion of what constitutes the biblical helpmate and the consequent false teaching on the subject, the women's problems have resulted. However, I don't agree with any solutions which suggest running away from the home in order for the woman to find her self-identity. Self-identity is not found in isolation, but in relationship.

Another emotional reaction has arisen from many well-meaning Christian women who defend the doormat life-style. This is a very popular approach today within the Christian movement. There are at least two lines of thought. One proposes woman as inferior to man; she must accept it and make the best of it! The other encourages women toward aggressiveness within their doormat life-style. The goal? It seems to be giddy women playing silly games in relating to their husbands. In some instances this is nothing more than a fantasy trip into childhood immaturity.

Misconceptions of Helpmate

Most of what is portrayed as *submission* is absolute distortion. There are three primary misconceptions regarding a "submissive" helpmate.

"Slave Girl"

This is the image of the girl locked in her house with a ball and chain attached to her foot. Her life is basically dull and uninteresting.

"Speechless"

In this case the woman is forbidden to say a word—especially that which may be contrary to the boss. She is constantly awaiting the "master's" next breath to direct her.

"Brain on Shelf"

Notice that her brain is equal to mustard and pickles! The woman is not permitted to think at all. Even if she were allowed, she would probably be unable to do so. *All of these are indeed misconceptions!*

Meaning of Helpmate

Submission is a biblical concept used in all relationships. Submitting to one another is characteristic of Christian conduct. It's not an invitation to be stomped on! It's voluntarily lifting another above yourself to serve him or her. It's a beautiful concept!

In this general realm of submission a husband and wife are to submit to one another—to lift the other up and to serve one another. This is why Paul begins his most lengthy discussion on marital responsibilities after he has stated the general principle of submission: "Be subject to one another" (*see* Ephesians 5:21). It's within this context of *mutual submission* that the husband's and wife's responsibilities are given. A general principle still must be applied in the specific.

In defining *helpmate* there are two things it is not. First, it is not a status of inferiority, but of voluntary subordination. Subordination is the key that releases God's fullness in both lives! The same principle is found in the Trinity (*see* 1 Corinthians 11:3). The husband is the head of the wife in the same way the Father is the head of Christ. Yet Christ and the Father are equal and one! Obviously there cannot be two leaders. The purpose of subordination is to allow two people to function as a team to complement one another instead of compete with one another.

Second, being a *helpmate* is not primarily an action but an attitude. The verbal aspect may or may not be present. Many women claim to be subordinate because they actually did what pleased their husbands. However, if you were to ask the husband, he would say she wasn't submissive at all. The difference in perspective lies in the fact that she was thinking in terms of action, while he was looking for a proper attitude along with the action.

Model of Helpmate

As with the man, Jesus is also the model for the woman's responsibility as helpmate. First, Jesus was in total submission to the Father and gave up every right He had. Even though equal with the Father, He ". . . did not regard equality with God a thing to be grasped" (Philippians 2:6). In the same way the wife should submit to God through her husband and give up her rights:

> Wives, be subject to your own husbands, as to the Lord. For the husband is the head of the wife, as Christ also is the head of the church, He Himself being the Savior of the body. But as the church is subject to Christ, so also the wives ought to be to their husbands in everything.
>
> Ephesians 5:22–24

After hearing that passage many women may say, "But you don't know my husband!" "You don't know Harry as I know Harry!" Peter has a direct answer to that common reaction:

> In the same way, you wives, be submissive to your own husbands so that if any of them are disobedient to the word, [Even if it is Harry!] they may be won without a word by the behavior of their wives.
>
> 1 Peter 3:1

Here again we see the principle commonly taught by Jesus— you must lose yourself to find yourself. As the woman dies to herself and submits to her husband she begins to find herself within that relationship. To insist and demand your rights will ultimately lead to the loss of them. Jesus warns us not to be caught up in the world's principle of finding life, because its end is destruction! Instead, you are to find fulfillment by losing your life. Learn to live fully by dying to yourself in submission to your husband. (This is the counterpart to the husband's death to self and giving himself up for his wife.)

There is a phrase that helps in defining *total submission;* it is "no resistance." Once a decision has been made, there should be "no resistance." A constant, gnawing resistance against your husband will push him into a corner, forcing him to either snap back at you or retreat altogether.

I have taken my family out to dinner quite often in a spur-of-the-moment decision. As we begin driving I'll usually say, "Honey, where would you like to eat?" "Oh, I don't care. You decide!" After a few seconds of thought I suggest, "Let's go to Taco Inn!" My wife responds, "Taco Inn? Do you really want to go there?" I then calmly offer another suggestion which precipitates more critical resistance. After a few rounds of this, you realize that this would have been a good day for fasting. Total submission involves no resistance.

Second, Jesus sought to glorify the Father (*see* John 13:31, 32). Similarly, the wife should seek to be the glory of her husband. Paul makes it clear in writing to the Corinthians that ". . . the woman is the glory of man" (1 Corinthians 11:7). What does it mean to be the *glory* of something? It means to reflect or reveal something or someone. Your husband's love is to set you apart to be a "glorious" woman. Now you are to cooperate by seeking to be that "glorious" woman through total submission. The cycle might look like this:

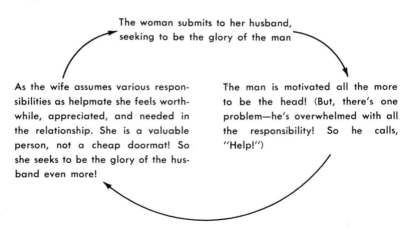

The woman submits to her husband, seeking to be the glory of the man

As the wife assumes various responsibilities as helpmate she feels worthwhile, appreciated, and needed in the relationship. She is a valuable person, not a cheap doormat! So she seeks to be the glory of the husband even more!

The man is motivated all the more to be the head! (But, there's one problem—he's overwhelmed with all the responsibility! So he calls, "Help!")

It's a beautiful combination! She is seeking to be the glory of the man by total submission, and the man is loving her sacrificially to the point of elevating her to be a glorious woman.

I know what you're thinking. *What if it's only a one-way relationship? What if I'm doing my part, but my mate doesn't even budge?* There are many ways of approaching a "one-way marriage." We'll discuss it in this chapter, and then in chapters 6 and 7 of Part Three the "dynamic duo" of love and blessing will be offered as an effective answer. But let's not get bogged down with your mate. You're responsible for your actions before God. Let's continue sharpening the focus on your responsibility!

Third, Jesus sought to trust the Father in His acts of submission. Realizing that God is the Designer of the family, the wife should endeavor to place her complete trust in God and His Design. In other words your total trust is not to be placed in your husband, whose commitment and concern for you could change, but in God, who is more concerned about you than you are. Merely to say "trust in God" can be a very empty saying. God doesn't leave us hanging in midair trying to trust Him. He normally gives an objective action step for us. For the wife to "trust in God" she is to actively submit to her husband. "For in this way in former times the holy women also, who hoped [trusted] in God, used to adorn themselves, being submissive to their own husbands" (1 Peter 3:5).

Trusting God and obeying your husband as God's representative authority in the home is where true security lies. God is not a male chauvinist, out to subjugate all women under all men. His Design is for all to experience fulfillment and full expression in life. His Design calls for one head and one helpmate—two distinct and equal responsibilities. This is the way He planned it! This is the way it works best! Anything other than this design short-circuits the full expression of life.

Fourth, Jesus sought to please the Father. In the same way, a successful wife seeks to love and please her husband. "She does him good and not evil All the days of her life" (Proverbs 31:12). You must be a student of your husband. What are his needs? What does he really enjoy? This will take some creativity and surprise. Early in our marriage Carol began a practice that has been a real lift to me. When I come home from the office, she and our girls are all dressed up nicely to greet me. (This isn't the king-arriving-home routine. We don't have the slipper and

newspaper bit at our house during the "valley of the shadow.")
No matter how worn out I am from the day's pressures this
greeting is refreshing!

Just think for a moment what many husbands go through in
a typical day in relation to their wives. The husband leaves home
for work; his wife sends him on his way. The husband carries a
vision of his wife to work. Her roller-and-pin-curl system gives
the appearance of being wired for sound. She's wearing a ten-
year-old robe, full of rips and snaps, with only two buttons
surviving. She has a new one in the closet, but just refuses to
give up the sentimental standby. As the husband arrives at his
work he notices that there isn't another woman in the world who
looks like his wife did this morning. Now actually the morning
scene isn't so bad, because that is an accepted part of life. The
real problem occurs when the husband arrives home and his
wife looks a little more tattered than she had appeared to be
early that morning.

Another thing my wife does that I enjoy is that she secretly
sends love notes in my suitcase when I travel to a conference.
She uses the element of surprise as she creates these "juicy" little
notes and hides them in my suitcase periodically. If she would
send a note on every trip I take, it would begin to lose its effect.

In addition to suggesting the use of creativity and surprise in
loving and pleasing your husbands, I want to insert a caution.
Be careful of being too "practical." Women have a tendency to
operate under the philosophy that anything less than pure practicality is wasteful. There are some things which seem wasteful
yet can be an important ingredient in solidifying your marital
relationship. This more than compensates for any "waste." It's an
investment in your marital oneness!

Fifth, Jesus was totally at one with the Father (*see* John
17:21). Any responsibility can be assumed by the wife as long as
there is a recognition of God's representative authority in the
home. The wife can handle the finances, but the husband still
functions in the responsibility of headship. She may do anything,
but the husband is the head of everything in that home. As the
relationship between husband and wife grows, each should seek
to become increasingly identified with the other's role and re-

sponsibilities. Thus the man and woman function more as a team —and enjoy it!

Mandate for Helpmate

Basically, the mandate for the helpmate is to submit to the husband in everything. In everything? Does that mean *everything?* What is the boundary of total submission? The principle is: *total submission without personal sin.* There are two striking illustrations of this principle in the Bible.

The first is that of Abraham and Sarah. Abraham lied to Pharaoh in telling him that Sarah was his sister and not his wife. Abraham's lie certainly would be described as disobedience to the Word. Sarah could have interrupted the conversation and let Pharaoh know she was really Abraham's wife. She had every reason to do so! Because of Abraham's lie, she knew she would be placed in Pharaoh's harem and probably be in his bed that night. Instead of actually telling Pharaoh herself, she could have gently nudged or glanced at Abraham to show her disapproval of his sin. This would have been a more subtle way of getting the truth to Pharaoh. Contrary to the natural response of a wife in this circumstance, Sarah submitted totally to Abraham, even in the objectionable venture, and God delivered her. However, if Sarah had been placed in the position of going to bed with Pharaoh, the only right thing she could have done would have been to refuse. It is at the point of personal sin that a woman must refuse to obey her husband. *The line of authority is not a line of access to God. Everyone is responsible for his own sin before God.*

The second illustration of this principle is that of Ananias and Sapphira (*see* Acts 5). Ananias lied to the church leaders concerning the price of some land he sold. In this particular situation the lie was directly against God as well. Since Ananias continued with his lie, he was struck dead by God. When Sapphira came in later, Peter asked her the price of the land to see what she would say. Here was her chance. It was good to submit to her husband even in the midst of his life, but now she was given the opportunity to tell the truth. This was not an issue of submission but an issue of personal responsibility before the Lord. She chose to lie and, like her husband, was struck dead. If she had chosen to tell the truth, she would have remained alive as a living testimony to the principle of total submission without personal sin. Instead, her death is a testimony to her failure to live up to her individual responsibility to God.

The question arises, "When can I disobey?" In every conceivable line-of-authority relationship there is a time to obey and a time to disobey. The only time disobedience becomes an option is when you are asked to do something directly contrary to Scripture. What you "feel the Lord is leading you to do" is not a reliable guide. Numerous rules and lists of sins that cannot be found in the Bible frequently form the focal point of the Christian's life-style.

At one Bible-study group I met a most interesting woman. She walked up after the study and said, "I'm sure you'll agree with me [With this kind of opening I'll either lose a friend or move into heresy.] when I say that God wants me here at this Thursday-morning Bible study."

"Well, I'm sure He is happy with your presence here."

She continued, "Even though my husband forbids me to come I sneak out in order to obey the Lord's Word. I've just been led by so many verses. You know the ones I mean."

I realized I had a real winner on my hands. I asked if she could find a couple of those verses that had convinced her to sneak out to the Bible class. She eagerly complied with my request. She sat over in the corner of the dining room and began to search diligently in her concordance. After most of the women had gone, she approached me with a somber look on her face.

"You're a minister, aren't you?"

"Yes."

"And you've probably read the Bible through a few times, haven't you?"

"Yes, I have."

"Have you ever read the verses I'm referring to?"

"No, I can't say that I have."

"That's what I thought," she said sadly.

She genuinely believed she had the God-given right to disobey her husband in this matter, until she failed to find those verses she just "knew" were in the Bible. Attendance at ladies' Bible-study groups does not even begin to be a biblical command!

For the sake of illustration, let's look at a situation where the husband asks the wife to do something that is clearly contrary to God's Word. Suppose your husband asks you to engage in wife-swapping, which is definitely wrong biblically. Your initial reaction should not be to explode. Instead, try calmly to ask yourself why he wants to engage in wife-swapping. Could it be that he wants something more sexually than what he is experiencing with you? After discerning the real reason behind the request, suggest a creative way of meeting his basic need without contradicting Scripture. In this specific instance you must overwhelm your husband sexually—meet his needs creatively. If done properly, he won't want to swap you with anybody!

Another sticky situation arises when a husband tells his wife she can't go to church. The Bible clearly states that we are not to "forsake the assembling of ourselves together" (see Hebrews 10:25). Yet the wife is to submit to her husband. I've counseled eleven cases such as this. In each case the real reason why the husband stopped his wife from attending church was because of her "preaching ministry" in the home. He was tired of hearing her preach, so he sought to cut off the source of her preaching. I suggested to each of these ladies to shut down the preaching ministry in the house and to not attend church for three or four Sundays. Then they were to ask their husbands if they could go to church. In every case (because his real reason for putting a stop to church attendance was removed) the husband allowed his wife to return to church. In fact a couple of them acted surprised their wives hadn't been going and encouraged them as never before.

The beauty of total submission is something to behold. Peter expresses it in his first letter:

> And let not your adornment be external only—braiding the hair, and wearing gold jewelry, and putting on dresses; but let it be the hidden person of the heart, with the imperishable quality of a gentle and quiet spirit, which is precious in the sight of God. For in this way in former times the holy women also, who hoped in God, used to adorn themselves, being submissive to their own

husbands. Thus Sarah obeyed Abraham, calling him lord, and you have become her children if you do what is right without being frightened by any fear.

1 Peter 3:3–6

The holy women who hoped in God adorned themselves (made themselves beautiful) by being submissive to their own husbands. Note that they adorned themselves not by submitting to all men but to their own husbands.

Of all the words that could have been used to describe the beauty of a woman's submission to her husband, the Lord chose a special one. He said it is *precious*. Another way to put it is "very expensive." This term is only used to describe a very few things that are most valuable to the Lord Himself. Can you visualize the Lord walking through His universe? As He walks He makes a comment concerning everything He has created—the stars, planets, animals, flowers, mountains. Then when He comes to the woman who is submissive to her husband (realizing she is not a doormat to be trampled upon, but a significant person responsible to God), He stops and says, "This is very expensive! She's precious!" Now for me to say something is expensive means very little. But for the God of the universe to say that something is expensive—that's expensive!

5

Priorities Are for People

Charles R. Buxton was the one who first said, "You will never 'find' time for anything. If you want time you must make it." Another said, "We are always complaining that our days are few, and acting as though there would be no end to them." We are all given the same amount of time. It is for us to decide how to spend it.

Priorities are referring to quality of time more than quantity. A priority item is an important one that must precede something else. Most people are too busy or are under extreme pressure to get things done. With few exceptions each one is wrestling with what to do next rather than with what is to be done ultimately.

We need a priority grid in order to make decisions that will produce peace and not pressure. Some of the most intense pressures in life are created by the inability to say No! with confidence that you are right. The result? Either a person is intimidated into saying yes to something that warranted a no, or he is burdened down with guilt after blurting out an unsettled no. Either way is pressurized. There is the pressure of doing too much, or the guilt of saying No!

A proper priority grid will free you from unnecessary pressures. I used to feel guilty for taking a day off or turning a ministry request down. But not any more! I have a new freedom to say No! based on my priority grid.

Although the Bible doesn't set forth a priority grid for us in five or six steps, such a grid can be constructed from the Bible with an understanding of various passages. The most basic of these passages is John 15. Here Jesus instructs His men concerning the relationships of life in three general categories. In verses 1–11 He discusses the believer's relationship with Christ Himself. He uses the figure of the vine—Jesus—and the branches—believers. This relationship is to be characterized by abiding in Him. In verses 12–17 is the believer's relationship with other believers. This relationship is to be characterized by loving one another. In the last section (18–27) Jesus describes the world's hate and disgust at believers because of their identification with Him. In verses 26, 27 He says: "When the Helper comes . . . He will bear witness of Me, and you will bear witness also, because you have been with Me from the beginning." This is the believer's relationship with the world, characterized by bearing witness of Jesus.

These three categories of relationships are used throughout the New Testament and in each case are offered as priority relationships. In John 15 the most important action for the believer is to abide in Christ. Then he is to actively love other believers and bear witness to the world. The greater his relationship with Christ the better his relationships with other believers. The greater his relationship with Christ and other believers the more effective his relationship to the world as a witness for Christ.

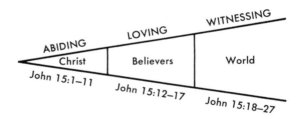

A proper priority grid cannot be developed without an understanding of these basic relationships emphasized in the Bible.

Other passages that add insight into priorities are found in the pastoral epistles of 1 and 2 Timothy and Titus. Paul lists qualifications for spiritual leadership and ministry. These qualifications are primarily qualities of life-style rather than abilities. They can easily be placed into the three categories of relationships that Jesus discussed in John 15. These are qualities in relationship to Jesus, in relationship to fellow believers (including family), and in relationship to the world. All of these qualify a person for ministry to others. Although these are specifically speaking of elders, deacons, and deaconesses, they serve as excellent guidelines for setting up a biblical priority grid.

Priority 1   *The cultivation of a personal relationship with the Lord.* This is your walk with God—not your ministry for Him. For quite some time I've been disturbed at how religious we are at times. We relate to the nonbeliever that Christianity is not a religious system of do's and don'ts, but that it is a relationship with God. Then as soon as a person becomes a believer we force him into being very religious. "You must come to these services. Then there is a prayer group which meets on Thursday that you should attend." "Oh, yes, you need to have a quiet time—just five or six minutes a day will be fine. Just be sure to check in with the Lord." These, and many, many more, swamp the new believer in "religiosity" and rob him of the natural development of a relationship with God. Suppose I were to tell you that I have an outstanding relationship with my wife, and the way it works is like this: at 6:30 in the morning we wake up; I say to my wife, "Honey, tonight from 6:00 to 6:30 is your time with me—be there!" That is not a relationship! At best it's an acquaintance! It seems that throughout Christianity too many are experiencing a "relationship" with God that is only an acquaintance—a nod to God at religious moments or at crisis points.

Cultivating a relationship with God is like any other relationship. There must be communication: talking (prayer to God) and listening (through God's written revelation). The more you communicate the more you know about Him and what pleases Him. So you seek to please Him by doing His will.

Priority 2   *The cultivation of a personal relationship with your mate.* After your relationship with God, the second most important relationship is with your mate. Many men find it easy to slip their vocation or ministry into this slot. On the other hand, women frequently place their children or home in this place.

For a long time in our marriage I didn't take a real day-off, because "I was in the ministry." As my conference schedule and counseling load continued to increase, the pressures on my wife and our relationship were overwhelming. Even though I thought the Lord's work may not be accomplished without my seven-day-a-week input, I decided to try a real day-off. No office mail or calls! No counseling over the phone! No preparation of messages! No writing of books or articles! It's amazing to me what happened. The Lord's work has continued, and my ministry is more effective. My wife is more excited about life, and our relationship has become more creative and refreshing!

I've talked with many men over the years who complain of their wives being extremely negative and naggingly resistant when the husband wants to go out with the guys—hunting or golfing or playing tennis. In such cases the wife is not down on hunting or golfing or tennis but is screaming for attention to the priorities of the marriage. In each situation I've counseled the man to evaluate and rework his priorities—emphasizing his need to cultivate an intimate, personal relationship with his wife. After laying this foundation of a relationship, the wife loses her need to be resistant and negative. In some cases she may even be excited about your activity. (More on this priority will be discussed in Part Three.)

Priority 3   *The cultivation of a personal relationship with your children.* Without a doubt the three most important aspects of parenthood are relationship, relationship, and then relationship. I'm convinced that parents could fail miserably in the area of discipline, being either too permissive or too authoritarian, and still succeed if there is a healthy relationship.

Although priorities are referring to *quality* of time more than quantity of time, be careful not to use that as a cop-out in this relationship. Relationships take time, so take the time to relate to each child individually every week.

Priority 4   *The cultivation of personal relationships inside the body of Christ.* Just as there is aloneness that is "not good" within the marital relationship, so there is aloneness within the body of Christ. Paul makes it clear in his letter to the Ephesian church that normal spiritual growth only takes place as each individual part of the body is fitted together and functions properly.

The Lord primarily touches or ministers to people's needs through His Word and through people. Just as we are to receive our mates as a gift from God to complete us, so are we to receive other members of the body of believers as gifts of God to us. Notice that there is a difference between "accepting" a person as he/she is and "receiving" a person as an ambassador of God (a believer-priest) to us.

Jesus viewed this priority so highly! He said that if this priority were in operation, the world would know that He was in reality sent by God!

Priority 5   *The cultivation of personal relationships outside the body of Christ.* Paul says we should have a "good reputation" with those outside the body of believers. Your vocation as well as your general conduct in business dealings would be included here. Your relationship to neighbors, relatives, organizations, and such are extremely important relationships. It's impossible to have intimate fellowship with unbelievers. We are told to separate ourselves, but not isolate ourselves, from them. We are separate in that believers have a standard of righteousness, light, and a relationship with God as opposed to the unbelievers' unrighteousness, darkness, and no relationship with God. We are to be open Bibles for them to read and examine so that they might find the God of the universe.

Priority 6   *The cultivation of personal ministry relationships.* The first five priorities qualify you for ministry to others in the more formal sense of the word. This may consist of teaching Bible studies or training sessions.

Unfortunately, this priority often is misplaced upward to a higher position on the priority list. Somehow it seems so easy to justify ministry activity at any cost. In a certain sense that may be true. But there is no justification possible when the cost may be your relationship with God or your family. You are disqualified from ministry if your first four priorities aren't in order.

Priorities free you to live according to God's game plan for marriage—free you to experience a maximum marriage.

III

Battle Scars or Blessings?

6

Love Is a Four-Letter Word

The basic ingredient of most marital problems is lack of communication. Every commitment made to God and to one another is put to the test at the level of communication. This is the point of contact between two people where the man and woman either enjoy their relationship by responding properly or endure it by reacting improperly.

Love and blessing are the two foundations of communication. All forms of communication between husband and wife must include them as basic working principles. The principle of love opens the door to communication in an active sense. Blessing opens the door to communication in a reactive sense (to be discussed in chapter 7).

What is the definition of *love?* *Love* is a four-letter word consisting of two consonants—*L* and *V*, two vowels—*O* and *E*, and two fools—you and me! Well, you may not define it in this way; but however you define it, true love was never meant to be passive. After the honeymoon is over many marriages are hit with the same problem. Staleness! The love that once burned with excitement grows cold. It burns out.

A good illustration of this stale relationship is that of the Joneses. Mrs. Jones just wasn't talking much anymore to her husband. So he decided she needed counseling. After nine weeks the counselor was baffled! On the tenth week the desperate counselor asked Mr. Jones to accompany his wife to the session. Once they were seated in the office the counselor stood up, walked around his desk to Mrs. Jones, and kissed her on the cheek. Mrs. Jones instantly began to come alive, hugged her husband, and told him all that had been happening over the past three months. Mr. Jones was shocked! He took the doctor into the other room and asked,

"I don't understand—what happened?" "Don't you see," the doctor blurted out, "your wife needs this kind of treatment Monday, Wednesday, and Friday!" Mr. Jones scratched his head in confusion and said, "Well, I can get her here on Monday and Wednesday, but I can't make it on Friday." Obviously, Mr. Jones missed the point. The doctor didn't want to administer the treatment, he wanted Mr. Jones to do that!

The little things in life demonstrate love so effectively. I can take my wife out to a nice steak dinner. When it's all over I'll ask, "Did you like it?" Her reply is, "I liked it, but I feel kind of sick. I ate too much." Now I spent all that money to make my wife sick. During the summer months you can buy a dozen roses for a dollar or so on nearly every major street corner. When I pick up a bunch of these roses and use the old behind-the-back trick at the door, my wife goes into ecstasy. For twenty dollars I make her sick—for one dollar she is overwhelmed! It's just a sound investment—little things in life demonstrate love best.

Explanation of Biblical Love

There is so much confusion in our world today concerning *love.* Most marital relationships have a wrong picture of love. Have you ever said, "I love oranges"? Exactly what do you mean by that? You are actually saying, "Oranges do something for me." However, after you have squeezed everything you like out of the orange, you will throw away the peelings. This is the same concept of love that many take as a basis for marriage. So when a person says *I love you* he or she really means, "You do something for me. After I squeeze all I want out of you, I will discard you, even as I threw away the orange peelings." Now there is nothing wrong with being attracted to the one you love and excited that he or she "does something for you," but that is not a proper foundation for marriage.

Biblical love is not getting all you can from another person but giving all you can. It is not conditional on what your lover does for you but is totally unconditional. One Greek word for *love* is *agape,* which translated means to commit yourself to seek the best for the object loved. It's committing yourself to give to another.

The most precise and dynamic statement of biblical, agape love is found in 1 Corinthians 13:4–7:

> Love is patient, love is kind, and is not jealous; love does not brag and is not arrogant, does not act unbecomingly; it does not seek its own, is not provoked, does not take into account a wrong suffered, does not rejoice in unrighteousness, but rejoices with the truth; bears all things, believes all things, hopes all things, endures all things.

Let's look at definitions of each of the terms describing *agape love* and begin to think of the application into the marriage. (Be prepared for painful conviction!)

Love is patient. Love enables you to endure offense from your mate, even though there is a tide of emotion welling up within you demanding that you retaliate.

This is the kind of patience that waits, prays for the reformation of your mate, and keeps you from lashing out in resentment against his or her conduct. Love will suffer many slights and neglects from the beloved and wait to see the kindly effects of such patience on him or her.

Love is kind. It responds with kindness when ill-treated. It seizes on opportunities to demonstrate tenderness and goodwill.

Love is not jealous. Love is never displeased at the successes or blessings that come to the mate. Envy sprouts from a relationship of competition and comparison.

Love does not brag. Love never tries to show off and brag about itself. There is no outward display of boasting. Never brag about your strengths in order to magnify your mate's weaknesses: "I don't ever have this problem." or "You don't see me doing that kind of thing, do you?" To love your mate involves esteeming him or her above yourself.

Love is not arrogant. Arrogance is an inner attitude of pride that stems from man-worship, a knowledge of Scripture apart from application—"superspirituality." One mate should never communicate that the other is "out of it" spiritually. It's so easy to intimidate—love does not do that.

Love does not act unbecomingly. Love does not behave in an unmannerly way, according to society's dictates of manners. A very simple yet destructive way of behaving unmannerly is to poke fun at or cut your mate down in public—or in private, for that matter!

Love does not seek its own. Love never seeks for its own interests—only for those of the mate. Be an ardent student of your mate's interests and take some positive action in those areas.

I like all sorts of sports, but there is one I've never even classified as a sport—hiking. I mean tennis, basketball, and golf are unquestionably great sports. But hiking? It seems so meaningless to me—aimlessly wandering around through a woods. My wife's favorite "sport" happens to be hiking. It's been so difficult to get her interested in something like tennis. But my difficulty was caused by my "seeking my own." One day I woke up to this and said, "Let's go hiking!" "Hiking?" "Yeah, let's go out and aimlessly wander through some woods!" (I almost lost my good effort with that last statement.) You know, that small action opened her up to participate in some *genuine* sports activities with me. Love does not seek its own.

Love is not provoked. It doesn't become bitter or resentful as a result of continuous irritations or offenses and will not respond to offenses with touchiness or anger.

Love does not take into account a wrong suffered. Love doesn't take evil into account when offended; it doesn't consider evil as a debt owed (something that must be "paid back"), and it never imputes evil motives to others.

Love does not rejoice in unrighteousness. Love never takes pleasure in the misfortunes that befall one's mate; it never has a "serves-him-right" attitude. You should not reflect an attitude of joy when your mate suffers the consequences of his or her offense or failure—even if you told them so.

Love rejoices in the truth. Love rejoices when truth is clearly presented and feels an inward joy and desire to respond to it. Heated arguments are normally a result of trying to win rather than seeking to find the truth and rejoicing in it. There is one time I don't want to rejoice in the truth—that is when my wife and I disagree, and she's more right than I am. This is the time I put on the righteous airs and say, "We really shouldn't argue about it. That's silly. Let's just drop the subject!" I know, if we continue, she will be proven right. On the other hand, the time I love to rejoice in the truth is when I'm more right than my wife; of course, my motive isn't too righteous in this case.

Love bears all things. Love equips you both to endure offense from your mate and to put a cloak of silence over your sufferings so that your mate's offenses and misdeeds are not divulged to the world. As a ship keeps water out, so love keeps the world from knowing the possible wrongs your mate is committing against you. There are affairs within your marriage that should be kept within the confines of the home. Too often extremely personal marital matters are publicized without discretion in prayer groups, usually under the guise of concern or a prayer request. Each mate must be able to trust in the other. Love bears all things.

Love believes all things. Love chooses to believe the best about the person and always assumes his or her motives and intentions are pure. To trust in your mate gives him or her a feeling of self-worth and acceptance. This is a key to effecting positive changes in the one you love.

Take a single girl named Sally and ask her what she thinks of John. "Oh, John, he's alright. He's just another guy." Then you let it be known that John thinks Sally is a beautiful girl and he really likes her. Now ask Sally the same question about John. Her reply? "Oh, that John, he's got insight!" What pepped up her response? She felt vibrations of love from John and she couldn't help but respond. The same is true of love vibrations in the marital relationship, except in this case it's more of a necessity for oneness.

Love hopes all things. Love gives you a confident expectation, based on the provision of God, that the offenses committed by your mate will be rectified and his or her weaknesses ultimately will be corrected, even in the face of evidence to the contrary. You should continue to hope joyfully, even in times of discouragement.

Love endures all things. Patient endurance is the quality that proves love for God. It enables one to endure any trial with a confident and joyful heart, because of the personal discipline that will be developed and the blessing of God that will result. Divorce is not a manifestation of the love that endures all things. The essence of love is commitment!

First Corinthians 13 is referring to a life-style. The fact that all the verbs in this passage are in the present tense emphasizes that these characteristics of love are to be habitually, repeatedly shown. However, just because a person doesn't possess one of these qualities in every instance does not necessarily mean his life-style is contrary to the passage. It's a process of growth!

Establishment of Biblical Love

Jesus gave three steps to the church at Ephesus in order to reestablish their "first love" for the Lord (*see* Revelation 2:4, 5). I like to suggest these same steps for establishing a biblical-love relationship in marriage as well.

The first step is to *remember.* Remember how it used to be? No, not in most marital relationships. The "how it used to be" kind of love most likely was not biblical—agape—love. After three disastrous years of marriage, a woman came for counseling and complained of no love for her husband at all. She related a very sad conversation she had with her mother the day before they were to be married. After telling her mother that she didn't want to get married to this man because she knew her reasons for marriage were only sexual, her mother responded with, "If you embarrass your dad and me by not going through with this, we'll disown you!" She married him. Could you tell her to remember "how it used to be" and get any positive results? Hardly!

It's not remember "how it used to be," but remember biblical love—the fifteen dimensions of love we just defined. Since you are constantly being programmed wrongly concerning love—the "I love oranges" approach—you must reprogram your mind concerning the way love was meant to be. Reprogramming the mind is not an uncommon experience. The Bible refers to it as *meditation*. This process of reprogramming will assist you in remembering the best response—the biblical one—to make in relating to your mate.

The second step in establishing biblical love is to *repent*. Now that you know what to do, you must decide you are going to do it. You do what you want to do and what you commit your will to do. So decide you are going to love your mate—biblically!

The third step is to *return to the deeds you did at first*. This is the hard part. You must respond to the new knowledge you have obtained. Biblical concepts are never given in a vacuum. Action is always required; for example, faith without works is dead faith according to James. In the same way, love without demonstration is worthless. In order to move into action you might take one of the fifteen dimensions of love and design a simple demonstration of that concept toward your mate. It could be overwhelming!

7

Blessings on Your Head

The second foundational principle of the communication process is the principle of *blessing*. Blessing opens the door to communication in a reactive sense. This may be the most radical principle of human relationships. Love is revolutionary, but giving a blessing for an insult is most incompatible with what the human nature automatically wants to do!

The normal reaction to an insult is to respond with another one—only it must be more cutting. Biblical examples of insults are interesting. You may find your "spiritual gift" in this list:

> *Name-calling:* Acts 23:4
> *Sarcasm and ridicule:* John 9:28
> *A nagging wife:* Proverbs 25:24; 27:15
> *A contentious man:* Proverbs 26:21
> *Insult and abuse in general:* 1 Corinthians 5:1; 6:9

The insulting response will get you nowhere but into mini-warfare! The proper reaction is to respond with a blessing for an insult! After a lengthy discussion concerning proper conduct of the believer within various contexts, Peter uses the principle of blessing to sum up all relationships:

> To sum up, let all be harmonious, sympathetic, brotherly, kind-hearted, and humble in spirit; not returning evil for evil, or insult for insult, but giving a blessing instead; for you were called for the very purpose that you might inherit a blessing. For "Let him who means to love life and see good days Refrain his tongue from evil and his lips from speaking guile. And let him turn away from evil and do good; Let him seek peace and pursue it. For the eyes of the Lord are upon the righteousness, And His ears attend to their prayer, But the face of the Lord is against those who do evil."
>
> 1 Peter 3:8–12

What is a *blessing?* There are four ways the term is used in the Bible: (1) *The praise of God and Christ* (Revelation 5:12, 13; 7:12). What positive qualities in your mate can you praise? (2) *Benefits—gifts—bestowed* (Romans 15:29; Galatians 1:3). What benefits can you offer your mate? In what way can you be a blessing to him/her? (3) *Giving thanks to God for His gifts and favor* (Luke 1:64; 2:28; Mark 6:41). What qualities about your mate are you thankful for, and how can you communicate this to him/her? (4) *To call God's favor down upon* (Luke 6:28; Matthew 21:9). What specific areas of your mate's life should you pray that the Lord will bless? These are the blessings that should be rendered in response to the insults you receive.

The principle of rendering a blessing for an insult is common throughout the New Testament.

> Never pay back evil for evil to anyone. Respect what is right in the sight of all men.
>
> Romans 12:17

> See that no one repays another with evil for evil, but always seek after that which is good for one another and for all men.
>
> 1 Thessalonians 5:15

. . . and we toil, working with our own hands; when we are
reviled, we bless; when we are persecuted, we endure.

1 Corinthians 4:12

bless those who curse you, pray for those who mistreat you.

Luke 6:28

You have heard that it was said, "You shall love your neighbor,
and hate your enemy." But I say to you, love your enemies, and
pray for those who persecute you in order that you may be sons
of your Father who is in heaven; for He causes His sun to rise
on the evil and the good, and sends rain on the righteous and
the unrighteous. For if you love those who love you, what re-
ward have you? Do not even the tax-gatherers do the same? And
if you greet your brothers only, what do you do more than
others? Do not even the Gentiles do the same?

Matthew 5:43–47

Why a Blessing?

Why do we need to give blessings? Why not a "righteous" jab?
Rendering a blessing for an insult is far from normal for the
average person. However, if God designed the family, He certainly knows what makes it work best.

As always God doesn't leave us hanging over the edge of a cliff
in order to take a leap of faith into the cold darkness. In 1 Peter
3:9–12 four reasons why you should render a blessing are given.
First: ". . . for you were called for the very purpose that you
might inherit a blessing" (v. 9). The purpose of the Christian life
is wrapped up in the desire of God that believers might enjoy
the blessings of life. So a believer must give a blessing in order
to inherit a blessing.

Second: ". . . let him who means to love life and see good days
refrain his tongue from evil . . ." (v. 10). The one who gives a
blessing instead of an insult will have days free from frustration
and tension. Many people are burdened down with heaviness
brought about by wrong reactions toward others. Bitterness and
resentment eat away at people's insides, causing problems rang-
ing from ulcers to eventual death. Giving a blessing lifts that
burden!

Third: "For the eyes of the Lord are upon the righteous, and

His ears attend to their prayer . . ." (v. 12). The Lord will pro-
tect those who give a blessing and will hear their prayers. One
might tend to think that giving a blessing affords a perfect opportunity for a person to be taken advantage of. ("I might get
stomped on if I gave a blessing!") But the promise of the Lord
to the one giving the blessing refutes that idea.

At this point you may be wondering why Peter has failed to
mention the responsibilities of the one who is persecuting you.
It's intentional! It's more important to God that you learn how to
respond to hurt in a godly way than for you to be delivered from
the one who is hurting you. God wants us to view these situations
as part of a learning experience; instead of seeing them as a
prison of circumstances, we are to see them as opportunities to
grow to maturity. However, once you have responded the way
God wants you to by giving a blessing, God then promises that
He will begin to deal with the mate who is hurting you.

Fourth: ". . . But the face of the Lord is against those who
do evil" (v. 12). The person who refuses to give a blessing but
gives an insult must reckon with the Lord. The Lord will work
on him! Paul sheds some light on this concept in Romans:

> Never take your own revenge, beloved, but leave room for the
> wrath of God, for it is written, "Vengeance is Mine, I will repay,
> says the Lord." "But if your enemy is hungry, feed him, and if
> he is thirsty, give him a drink; for in so doing you will heap
> burning coals upon his head." Do not be overcome by evil, but
> overcome evil with good.
>
> Romans 12:19–21

In order for the Lord to work on the one doing evil, you must
get out of the way—"leave room for the wrath of God." Let God
work on the insulter by your giving a blessing—the Lord will do
a much better job than you could ever do.

How to Give a Blessing!

Jesus employed four steps in responding to insult, and we are
commanded to imitate them. (See 1 Peter 2:21–25.)

Step 1   *You are to have no personal offense (see* v. 22). You can't give a blessing to someone if you have unconfessed sin before God and between you and the offended. One evening Carol and I had an argument over something. In the midst of it all Carol became quite upset—more than I thought the situation called for. I left the room to allow the scene to cool off. I then returned with a blessing (expressing appreciation for a quality in her life). After I verbalized the blessing, Carol turned and said, "If that was meant to be a blessing, it isn't going to work!" I couldn't believe it! I said, "What do you mean?" Apparently without realizing it I cut her with some verbal jab (it's natural for me) while we were disagreeing. What she was saying is, "If you think you can give a blessing to me when you were the original offender, you're very mistaken!" Because I had offended her, I was disqualified in giving out blessings!

Step 2   *Purpose to render a blessing for the insult or hurt you have experienced (see* v. 23). Here's where the will enters in— decide you are going to give a blessing when insulted. Creatively seek the appropriate blessing by the use of the following questions:

What positive qualities about my mate can I praise him/her for?
What benefits could I bestow on my mate?
In what way can I be a blessing to him/her?
What qualities about my mate am I thankful for?
How can I communicate this to him/her?
What specific areas of my mate's life should I pray that the Lord
    will bless him/her in?

Obviously, the most difficult time to give a blessing is in the heat of the battle. It's probably better to walk away from the battle, for both to cool off emotionally. Then return with a genuine blessing.

Step 3   *Commit yourself and the situation to the Lord.* Thank Him for raising up this situation for the purpose of making you more Christlike (*see* Romans 8:28, 29; 1 Thessalonians 5:18). Then commit yourself to the Lord's keeping and vow to withdraw yourself from the battle so the Lord can begin to deal with your offender. Release the Lord to act by giving a blessing (*see* Romans 12:17–21).

Step 4   *Purpose to be willing to suffer in order to heal your offender* (*see* 1 Peter 2:24). When you give a blessing, all may not be resolved for a period of time. In fact, you may look like the fool or be hurt because of your position of blessing. Think of Christ! What were the results Christ achieved in following these four steps? Those who were astray returned to the Shepherd (*see* 1 Peter 2:25).

One woman faced with some of the worst insults I've ever witnessed gave some of the best blessings ever given. Her husband traveled nationally as a salesman. He came home eight to twelve days per month. He told her he came home only for sex with her; but in the same breath he related to her his various sexual exploits around the country. Even in front of the children he mentioned these other women. It was a tragic scene! No one would have faulted her for filing for divorce. But someone got to this woman before she did anything drastic and challenged her to heal her mate through being a blessing. It was a real test of how much she loved him. After three long years, he came home for good. Now the family is back together, better than ever before. Was it tough? It was hell on earth! Was it worth it? They couldn't be happier!

When you add *blessing* to the principle of *love,* you have a "dynamic duo" which will overwhelm anyone! A very frustrated and lonely woman came in for counseling. She complained of her husband who never stayed home. He went to five parties a week from which he repeatedly came home drunk—the other two nights he worked! I discussed with her how she could allow the Lord to work on him through love and blessing. I also suggested that she should go to a party with him. "And get drunk?" she said. "No, just go to the party!" When he arrived home that night he was immediately in shock; she was dressed beautifully. He said, "You don't want to go to the party tonight, do you?" "Yes, I'd like to." (That was his second shock!) They went to the party, and neither of them even had anything to drink. They just sat and talked to each other. When they were going to bed that evening, they began to make love. He stopped all of a sudden and said, "What have you been doing?" She proceeded to tell him, but he stopped her and said, "Never mind, just keep it up, I like it!" A week later she called and ecstatically said, "He's only been to two parties this week. I went with him to both of them, and he didn't get drunk. He talked to me. The rest of the week he's been home in the evenings talking to me! Can you believe it?" Caught up in her excitement I said, "I can't believe it!"

When your mate insults you, don't retaliate with an insult. Render a blessing, and let God deal with your mate—He'll do a much better job!

8

Where's Dinner?

Communication involves something more than words! Each word that is spoken conveys a certain disposition through tonal quality or facial and physical gestures. As a matter of fact, words may not even be necessary for a mood or disposition to be recognized. What we call *disposition* the Bible calls *spirit*. The spirit of a man communicates more than most people realize, which is the reason for the warning to "take heed then, to your spirit, and let no one deal treacherously" with his mate (*see* Malachi 2:15). There are certain things about your mate's spirit that sometimes really tick you off. It's crucial in the process of communication that you pay attention to your spirit and the spirit of your mate.

The goal of marriage is oneness. In a very real sense spiritual communication is the adhesive of marital oneness; so it's essential that a couple strive to achieve spiritual unity—the blending of two spirits together under God.

Formation of the Human Spirit

It's interesting to examine the spirit of a person. There are four dimensions of the spirit that specifically relate to the marriage relationship. The first is *mood*. This is by far the most common usage of the word *spirit* in the Bible. A *mood* is a pervading disposition or emotional feeling. It refers to a frame of mind or a state of feeling. The spirit of Christmas is the mood of the Christmas season. The Bible speaks of the moods of the human spirit under various categories: a wounded spirit, a revived spirit, a hardened spirit, an upright spirit, and others.

The second dimension of the human spirit is *motivation*. It's within the spirit that you find motivational drives, desires, and goals. This is the seat of proper and improper motives.

The third dimension of the human spirit is *perception*. *Perception* is how you view life and people. You can view life from God's perspective or from the world's perspective. If you view a person from the world's perspective he'll be a threat to you. If from God's perspective, you'll see a person with needs which must be met. Perception is also the ability to sense another's spirit. It's a sensitivity or an insensitivity to your mate.

The fourth dimension of the human spirit is *contact with God*. Jesus said: "that which is born of the [Holy] Spirit is [human] spirit" (*see* John 3:6). It's in the spirit of a man that he has contact with God or lack of contact with God.

The following diagram pictures the dimensions of the human spirit and how they seem to relate.

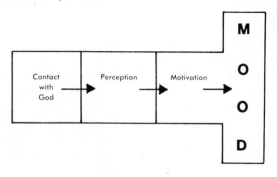

Contact with God or lack of it affects perception—how you view life, from God's perspective or the world's. In turn, how you perceive life directly affects motivation—your goals, motives, and desires. All of these flow into the mood—the disposition of a person.

How Spiritual Communication Is Broken

There are two ways by which spiritual communication is broken: a breakdown in the spirit itself, and a breakdown of specific attitudes. In the first one there can be a breakdown in any one or a combination of the dimensions of the spirit. There can be a breakdown in contact with God. One mate may have a personal relationship with God and the other may not. That will cause some conflict. Also there may be a situation where both have contact with God, but one is not open to God's direction. A breakdown in perception occurs when one is very insensitive to the other. Quite often I have counseled with men who said, "My wife just packed up and left me, and I don't have the foggiest notion why!" That's exactly the problem—he hasn't had the "foggiest notion" about his wife for a long time. He's lacking in perception as it relates to her. There can also be a breakdown in the area of motivation. One mate, a believer, says to the other who is not, "Let's give more money to the church." The unbeliever thinks, *The ten dollars we gave last year was entirely too much!* That's a breakdown in communication in the area of motivation—goals and desires. Then finally there can be a breakdown in the area of mood. The way things are said and the way things are not said can definitely cause a breakdown in communication.

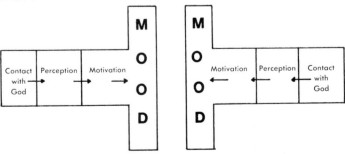

Not only is spiritual communication broken by a breakdown in the dimensions of the spirit itself, but also through a breakdown of specific attitudes. There are at least four which have significant power in causing disintegration in communication: non-acceptance, irresponsibility, selfishness, and an insulting attitude. The attitude of *nonacceptance* will affect the mood negatively. After you express something that is meaningful or exciting to you, nonacceptance might raise its head and the response is, "That's ridiculous!" Does that encourage you to open up and be more expressive with your mate? The attitude of *irresponsibility* is present when there is confusion of the roles, or role-reversal. This also does wonders for the mood or disposition of the relationship! The attitude of being *selfish*—the big "I" problem—destroys two-way communication because everything must revolve around one person. The *insulting* attitude borders on guerilla warfare! It constantly gnaws away at the relationship and is especially a hindrance to oneness.

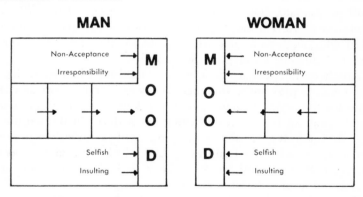

How Spiritual Communication Is Built

Step 1 *Establish contact with God.* You must establish contact with God together. Obviously this is impossible without each mate knowing God personally through the Lord Jesus Christ. Once you are each rightly related to God, the next step is to establish *together* a relationship with God. Some defeats and frustrations have been experienced by Christian couples in this attempt at oneness. Personal motivation doesn't seem to be the

problem in many cases. On the contrary, couples are often so
motivated that their times together with God contain a built-in
fizzle. Some particular reasons for the fizzle are that their meet-
ings together are too long, too frequent, and the studies too hard.
My wife and I have tried nearly everything and failed at most
all of them. In my first year of seminary I realized that Carol
wasn't getting all the fantastic "gems" that I was enjoying, so
I decided to set up a little curriculum (Timmons Theological
Seminary) just for her. I could teach her a course each semester
over the four years and she would be the most educated seminary
wife ever. We were to meet three times a week for two hours.
The first course was the study of the Books of Daniel and Revelation. (I was so enthusiastic!) In the first hour I did an overview
of Daniel. The response was not entirely what I anticipated; she
yawned and kept looking at her watch. After the overview, we
took a ten-minute break, but after about fifteen minutes she
hadn't returned. When I finally found her, busily folding the
clothes, she said, "Oh, is the break over already?" I then did an
overview of Revelation. Again her response was overwhelming!
(But who needs to be overwhelmed like that?) That experience
ended Timmons Theological Seminary!

Another failure occurred early in our ministry when we realized
our need to pray more together. We were highly motivated to
pray for the needs of many people we knew. So we decided we
would pray an hour a day, starting at six-thirty in the morning.
The first morning we started praying right on time; we prayed
and prayed and prayed and prayed. We looked up at the clock.
It was 6:40 A.M.; and we went back to bed. That experience
fizzled out after only three mornings.

To counteract the fizzle you must not stifle the motivation but
channel it sensibly toward your goal of experiencing mutual contact with God. The first sensible step in this direction is to make
your time together *short*. Hasty resolutions are made, with good
intentions, to pray together an hour a day or to study the Bible
for an hour before starting the day. But then these resolutions
come into conflict with the problems and interruptions of life.
There are: phone calls, children, guests, the failure of the alarm
to go off, the seeming impossibility of praying for a whole hour,

spending most of the time deciding what to study, and other such distractions. Discouragement sets in! The result? Another good resolution has been tried and found wanting. Try making your time with God short at first. There is nothing magical about an hour; maybe a half-hour would be better for you. You can always increase the time later.

A second sensible step toward establishing a meaningful time together is to make it *regular*. Regular doesn't necessarily mean daily or even every other day. Regular could mean weekly. (I think yearly might be taking advantage of the principle. That would hardly benefit anybody.) Set a regular time together which you can generally control and guard as your time together with the Lord. Carol and I have found one night per week is the best for us. Virtually nothing can interrupt that evening together. If, in a rare case, that night must be cancelled, another night in the same week is scheduled.

The third sensible step is to make your time with God *achievable*. Probably the greatest obstacle to mutual contact with God is leaping into some kind of study that is too difficult or not interesting to both mates. The content should be simple, interesting, and mutually beneficial. This is to be a time where you are learning about God and your relationship to him together. It's not a time for one to sit the other down to teach him/her spiritual gems, but a time of mutual encouragement and growth. A study in the Book of Proverbs, using various approaches, can be extremely practical. Numerous devotionals are available today. Guides for studying doctrines or books of the Bible are a good resource as well. Beware of becoming too theoretical. Force yourself to answer the question: *What does this mean to us?* There is no divine method of establishing time together with God, because people's needs and schedules vary so much. But whatever you do, establish a regular, meaningful contact with God— together!

Even more important than this, however, is to take advantage of spontaneous times with the Lord. In the midst of the everyday happenings of life, situations arise for which you need answers and direction. These are perfect times to search the Bible or seek the Lord in prayer to find His will. To fail to capitalize on these

golden opportunities is to miss the most practical application
of God's Word in real life.

Step 2 . *Build perception—walk in your mate's shoes.* There
are two differences in masculinity and femininity that each mate
should understand. The first difference is that men are basically
living in the *long-range* and women are basically living in the
immediate. If you aren't aware of this and sensitive to it, you are
in for some deep misunderstandings and disappointments.

An example of this difference happens frequently when I'm
excited about going some place. When I realized we had the
opportunity to go to Israel, I raced across town to tell my wife.
I ran into the house and screamed, "We're going to Israel for
a month!" Carol's normal response to that kind of exciting announcement is to pose a number of questions: "How can we
afford it? What about the children? What about the house? What
will we do with our car?" That's just like being stopped by a
bucket of ice water! But it's not entirely her fault. I caused much
of the problem by my insensitivity to her as a woman. She's
thinking of the immediate necessities of life, while I'm thinking
in a long-range, visionary fashion. What I should say in a situation like that is, "Honey, I've got a topic sentence and a few
things to follow. Topic sentence: We're going to Israel! Hold it,
there's more! It's paid for! I know where the children will stay.
The house will probably stay right here. The car will remain in
the garage." Now I've met the needs of the immediate so that
she can be free to get excited with me.

The second difference is that men are basically physical and
women are basically emotional. This doesn't mean that neither
of them thinks; nor does it mean that women are not physical,
nor men are not emotional. The most intimate door of communication with the man is physical and with the woman it is emotional. If a man wants to open up his wife most intimately, he
must relate to her through the emotions—empathizing with her,
treating her warmly and tenderly, and genuinely caring for her.
If a woman desires to open up her husband most intimately,
she must relate to him physically—sexually. The latter has been
grossly perverted! Many have observed this truth and proceeded

to twist it into saying that sexual communication is only one-way. They say that sex is only for the husband's enjoyment not the wife's. There is nothing further from the truth, as will be obvious from chapter 10, "Biblical Lovemaking."

"I've only got three more weeks, and then my marriage is over!" Here was a desperate case! This lady's husband announced to her in December that he would be leaving at the end of January. He declined to give any reasons. In fact, he clammed up after his announcement and retreated into a shell. "What can I do? He won't talk about it at all!" I told her I had an idea, but that I was sure she couldn't do it. She pleaded until she finally said, "I'll do anything to keep my family together." That was the level of commitment I needed. So I told her, "You need to go home tonight and overwhelm him sexually." She said, "Who, me?" I jokingly said, "Did you have anyone else in mind?" She continued, "I've just never done that before!" After convincing her that this sort of action was alright biblically, she consented to do it.

The next day she called me. "I can't believe it. He actually began to open up last night. There is something wrong at his office, but he didn't explain the entire situation fully. At least I know it's not just the home situation he's running from. What do you think I should do now?" "What do I think you should do? Again, lady, again!" Just three days later she called ecstatically, "He told me everything! We talked it all out; and I even offered a solution to the problem at the office, which he thought was the answer he needed. We've never had a better talk in the thirteen years of marriage!"

Step 3   *Effect changes in your mate through motivations.* You need to counteract any of the bad attitudes which may have hindered communication with new goals and commitments. To counteract nonacceptance make a commitment to completeness (chapters 1 and 2). To counteract irresponsibility make a commitment to accept the responsibility of head or helpmate (chapters 3, 4, and 5). To counteract selfishness make a commitment to agape-style love (chapter 6). To counteract the insulting attitude make a commitment to give a blessing to your mate (chapter 7).

Do you see what's happening? The game plan for maximum marriage is all fitting together to produce an intimate and enjoyable oneness.

Step 4 *Attend to your mood.* Another way to establish spiritual oneness is to pay attention to your mood and the mood of your mate. As we have seen, this is by far the most common meaning of the word *spirit* in the Bible. The Proverbs have much to say concerning mood as it relates to communication:

> A soothing tongue is a tree of life,
> But perversion in it crushes the spirit.
> Proverbs 15:4

> A joyful heart is good medicine,
> But a broken spirit dries up the bones.
> Proverbs 17:22

Principles concerning mood in communication are easily grouped under three phrases found in James 1:19: *quick to hear, slow to speak,* and *slow to anger.*

Be Quick to Hear

Listening involves shutting the mouth! This may be the most obvious of the principles, but it's also the most violated.

> When there are many words, transgression is unavoidable,
> But he who restrains his lips is wise.
> Proverbs 10:19

> The one who guards his mouth preserves his life;
> The one who opens wide his lips comes to ruin.
> Proverbs 13:3

> Even a fool, when he keeps silent, is considered wise;
> When he closes his lips, he is counted prudent.
> Proverbs 17:28

Create a nonthreatening climate. A threatening climate is easily created—even without words. A look or gesture that communicates *That's ridiculous!* is a normal way to threaten your mate. That is anything but being quick to hear!

> Through presumption comes nothing but strife,
> But with those who receive counsel is wisdom.
>
> Proverbs 13:10

Empathize, don't sympathize. Seek to understand the feelings rather than the words. To sympathize is to pat your mate on the back and feel sorry for him/her. To empathize is to identify with his/her feelings by becoming personally involved in them.

Ask questions for clarification. In the process of listening you may need to ask a question to be certain you understand properly. You might say, "You mean . . . ." But don't say, "You don't mean . . . !" You must demonstrate an openness as you inquire.

Slow to Speak

> Anxiety in the heart of a man weighs it down,
> But a good word makes it glad.
>
> Proverbs 12:25

Keep communication lines open. Whenever you feel tension in your communication you can dissolve it by laughing at yourself, verbalizing appreciation, projecting genuine concern, and asking meaningful questions. Unfortunately, in many marriages the most meaningful and creative question is How was your day? The normal encouraging answer is a dynamic Okay. What meaningful communication!

Avoid explosive words like always *and* never. The wife may say, "You never come home on time for dinner!" She is saying that he has never, not even once, been home for dinner on time. But he's thinking of the one time he did come home on time. The argument begins!

Avoid sarcasm, ridicule, innuendos. These do nothing but stir up anger.

> A gentle answer turns away wrath,
> But a harsh word stirs up anger.
>
> Proverbs 15:1

> Pleasant words are a honeycomb,
> Sweet to the soul and healing to the bones.
>   Proverbs 16:24

Avoid the "you have the same problem" reaction. When one mate accuses the other of some irresponsibility, the one accused usually refuses to discuss the charge. Instead he or she turns it back on the accuser and says, "But you are just as irresponsible in this other area when you . . . ." In this situation the real issues are not discussed at all. The couple just keeps score. No one really wants to win—just to keep the score even!

I'm a "Tab-aholic!" There's only one real problem with being a Tab-aholic—Tab bottles are left in the car, and bottles roll! Carol can't stand the rolling of bottles in the car, so my job is to keep the car free of Tab bottles. My daughter, Tammy, is a "raisin-freak." That's fine except that she misses her mouth often, and the backseat of the car is speckled with raisins, so my wife's job is to keep the backseat free from raisins.

One evening we were off to some friends for dinner. I was waiting in the car listening to the news when I saw a Tab bottle on the floor behind Carol's seat. Not wanting to admit my failure in the matter, I decided to wrap a cloth around it and lodge it under her seat so it wouldn't move.

We were running late, so I wasn't wasting any time scooting across intersections in our VW. All of a sudden a green light turned red instantly, without changing to yellow. (I'm sure you've seen those.) I slammed on the brakes! The crazy bottle worked itself loose, flew up, and hit Carol's foot. Well, there we were sitting at the red light. Carol didn't say a word. She just looked at me! Her spirit did the communicating! *A bottle just hit my foot! You know the bottle was to be removed from the car!* Instead of admitting my oversight I turned around toward the backseat and said, "I noticed there are still some raisins on the backseat." Be careful of the "you have the same problem" reaction!

Slow to Anger

> He who restrains his words has knowledge,
> And he who has a cool spirit is a man of understanding.
>   Proverbs 17:27

> A fool does not delight in understanding,
> But only in revealing his own mind.
>
> Proverbs 18:2

Your motivation should not be to win but to gain understanding. There is nothing wrong with true argument. The freedom to disagree is important. However, the purpose is to come to the true and proper understanding of a given issue. Most arguments in the home stem from competition and comparison. Therefore, each person is out to gain a victory—to win points. This is a futile exercise that constantly hacks away at the oneness of the relationship. Try to stop one another and each one state the other's argument.

Keep emotions under control. Arguments become quarrels when there is more heat (emotion) than light (understanding). Keep your voice down. Shouting encourages extreme emotional reaction without reflection on what is being said. Another way to trigger emotions is by any short, quick movements—for example, standing quickly and shoving the chair under the table. These quick movements stir up the emotions of your mate. Normally the mate will be moved to shouting. The shouting seems to indicate the one who lost control first, but in truth it's the one who triggered the shouting with short, quick movements of anger. When driving I sometimes show my anger by tramping on the accelerator. (It doesn't actually affect the speed of the car in a VW.)

> Be angry, and *yet* do not sin; do not let the sun go down on your anger, and do not give the devil an opportunity.
>
> Ephesians 4:26, 27

Make things right before sundown. Settle all arguments—at least to the point of agreeing to disagree—before going to bed. Too many carry the tension and frustration with them to bed and build up resentment that is not dealt with until an explosion occurs much later.

Spiritual communication is essential to oneness in marriage. It's just good strategy to strive for spiritual oneness by paying attention to your mate's spirit and to your own.

9

Biblical Lovemaking

Physical communication is the most intimate expression of marriage. Various studies demonstrate that the majority of couples divorcing today are doing so because of sexual problems. It's important to note that in most cases these sexual problems are symptoms of deeper problems. Because of the strong, natural drive toward sexual satisfaction, sex becomes the focal point of many marital conflicts. If there is a sense of competition, nonacceptance, role problems, lack of true, biblical love, or neglect in the area of spiritual oneness, it will be revealed within the sexual relationship. Sex is not the key to marital happiness but its most full expression.

Nevertheless, problems arise within that expression because of misunderstanding resulting from the lack of positive, directive teaching on the subject. Much of what young people learn about sex today is "picked up" in an unwholesome context and replete with misinformation. Most of the blame for the lack of teaching in the area of sex rests with the home and church. Both of these institutions are in existence for the purpose of training people how to live, but in each of them very little is discussed concerning sex. It's easy to comprehend why the impression that sex should not be discussed or that sex is dirty permeates the Christian world.

There are six biblical principles regarding sex. These general principles don't present the whole picture, complete with specifics of techniques or sexual problems. However, they are the most important underlying principles upon which an intimate sexual relationship is based.

Sex Is Good and of the Lord

Sex is not a hidden subject in the Bible. Nearly every book contains something about it. Two books in the Old Testament have the sexual relationship as their theme. The Bible is not down on sex, but is quite negative concerning a misuse of it. The negative is only present to guide you into a more positive, intimate relationship. In fact, God is so in favor of the oneness factor—physical and spiritual—that He uses the marital oneness to illustrate the relationship of Christ (Bridegroom) and the Church (Bride).

Extremists run rampant in every subject and sex is no exception. On the one hand, you'll find the puritanical philosophy which holds that a love relationship is fine, but sex is only for procreation. On the other hand, you'll encounter the *Playboy* philosophy—those who want the freedom to "enjoy sex with whomever we chose." Both are very wrong! The love relationship bound by marital commitment but devoid of sexual pleasure is not right! The best and most enjoyable relationship consists of both the marital bond of love and pleasurable sex.

Why did God design sex into marriage anyway? Obviously, the procreation of the human race is one reason. In Genesis 1 God says, "Be fruitful, multiply, and fill the earth" (*see* v. 28). In Genesis 2 another reason arises. It's the basis for completion of man—male and female, as discussed in Part Two. Adam was looking for a helpmate—a *completer*. The word literally means "according to his front presence." He wasn't searching just for a soul out there, but for a physical body as well. Another reason for God's design of sex in marriage is pleasure. Remember the Deuteronomy 24 passage?

> When a man takes a new wife, he shall not go out with the army, nor be charged with any duty; he shall be free at home one year and shall give happiness [cheer up sexually, not tell jokes] to his wife whom he has taken.
>
> Deuteronomy 24:5

This passage is commanding (in the Jewish law) a new couple to enjoy sex for a full year! (I'm glad I didn't say that! I'd be criticized for it!)

Probably the most complete illustration of God's attitude toward sexual love in marriage is the Old Testament book Song of Solomon. For centuries the book has been abused by Christian allegorizers who see the book primarily as a picture of Christ and the church. It is valid to say that the Song of Solomon presents a good picture of Christ and the church as any marriage should, but it is primarily speaking of a love relationship between husband and wife. Historically, this view of Christ and the church developed because of unchristian views about sex which suggested that sex was not holy. Therefore the literal, normal view of the book couldn't be accepted, because God would never have allowed a book about sex in marriage in the canon of Scripture.

The primary purpose of the Song is to present God's perspectives on sexual love in marriage. The book is highly intimate and yet set against an ethical background of monogamy and premarital chastity. The Song speaks definitively that sex in marriage is holy and pure before God and that any kind of sexual love between husband and wife is holy and beautiful before God.

The story of Song of Solomon is a simple love story. King Solomon, Israel's richest king, owns vineyards all over Syria—Palestine. One of these vineyards was located at Baal-hamon in the Galilean countryside. While visiting this vineyard one day, he met a country maiden, Shulamit. Shulamit captured Solomon's heart and he fell in love with her. For some time he pursued the courtship and made periodic visits to the north to see her at her country home.

Finally he asked her to marry him. Shulamit accepted, but only after serious consideration as to whether or not she really loved him and as to whether or not she could be happy in the palace of a king.

Solomon sends a wedding procession to bring his new bride to the palace in Jerusalem and the book opens as she is getting ready for the wedding banquet and the wedding night. The details of their first night are intimately but tastefully described.

The second half of the book deals with the joys and problems of their married life. Shulamit refuses Solomon's sexual advances one night and the king departs. Shulamit, realizing her foolishness gets up and tries to find him and eventually does. They have a joyous time embracing once again.

While she lived at the palace, the new queen often longed for the Lebanon mountains in which she was raised. She finally asks Solomon to take her there on a vacation and Solomon agrees. The book closes with her return to her country home and their enjoyment of sexual love in the mountains of Lebanon.

The Song speaks very specifically about sex in marriage through poetic symbolism. God could have spoken of such matters using accepted medical terms or slang words; but when medical terms are used a sense of awkwardness develops, and when slang is used an internal psychological censor causes us to react to what is being said. Consequently God avoided both problems by expressing these delicate things in the language of poetry and symbolism.

Let's listen in on Solomon and Shulamit at their wedding banquet, as described in the Song of Solomon 1:9–14.

> SOLOMON: To me, my darling, you are like
> My mare among the chariots of Pharaoh.

That doesn't sound too swift for a lover, does it? But she wasn't offended by it because it was a high compliment in that culture. The horse was a cherished companion of kings, not a beast of burden.

> SOLOMON: Your cheeks are lovely with ornaments,
> Your neck with strings of beads.
>
> CHORUS: We will make for you ornaments of gold
> With beads of silver.
>
> SHULAMIT: While the king was at his table,
> My perfume gave forth its fragrance.

The fragrance here is nard. This was a very expensive ointment. The Shulamite has anointed herself with this perfume and she sees the fragrance emitting from her to the king as an expression of her love reaching out to him. She's saying that Solomon brings out the best in her.

SHULAMIT: My beloved is to me a pouch of myrrh
Which lies all night between my breasts.

This refers to an oriental custom in which a woman would wear a sack of myrrh (a kind of perfume) around her neck in order to bring out a lovely fragrance all day long. She is saying that Solomon is to her like that pouch of myrrh. He has described her beauty. She responds and says that whatever beauty and charm she has, has been brought out by her lover. His love causes a fragrance to emit from her all day.

SHULAMIT: My beloved is to me a cluster of henna blossoms
In the vineyards of Engedi.

The vineyards of Engedi are surrounded by wilderness and the Dead Sea. She is saying that Solomon is to her like the ornamental henna blossoms in contrast to the desolate area roundabout. He stands out like that and therefore makes her stand out beautifully. Later that evening, in the bridal chamber, they continue to express their love (vs. 15–17).

SOLOMON: How beautiful you are, my darling,
How beautiful you are!
Your eyes are like doves.

SHULAMIT: How handsome you are, my beloved,
And so pleasant!
Indeed, our couch is luxuriant!
The beams of our houses are cedars,
Our rafters, cypresses.

She's excited about the way Solomon had the bedroom decorated for her—cedars of Lebanon, cypresses. Most bedrooms today look like one big closet. It's the most unromantic room of the house! Get rid of the spotlight in the middle of the room. Why not try colored lights or candlelight. Everyone looks better by candlelight! The story continues in chapter 2.

SHULAMIT: I am the rose of Sharon,
The lily of the valleys.

The Shulamite explains why she is so appreciative of Solomon's efforts to make their bedroom like the countryside which she loves. It's because she is like a tender flower which has grown up in the quietness of rural life (2:1). She is humbly describing herself as a meadow flower. Understandably she had fears of being out of place, a common meadow flower in King Solomon's palace.

SOLOMON: Like a lily among the thorns,
So is my darling among the maidens.

Solomon picks up on her statement and heightens the image. He says that compared to her, all the other girls in the kingdom are as thorns (v. 2).

SHULAMIT: Like an apple tree among the trees of the forest,
So is my beloved among the young men.
In his shade I took great delight and sat down,
And his fruit was sweet to my taste.

They are apparently actively involved in lovemaking at this point (v. 3). The apple (and the symbol of fruit) is a frequent symbol in the Near East for love. It's used throughout the Song for sexual love. In other words, she is expressing to Solomon what a good lover he is. She enjoyed making love with Solomon!

The entire book is overwhelming in its theme that sex is good and even "the very flame of the Lord" (see 8:6). We'll return to the Song of Solomon later.

Sex Is More Than Physical

There's a very simple principle that must be verbalized here. When you see someone coming toward you, nine times out of ten there's a person inside that body! (I say nine times out of ten, because I've met some strange bodies that made me wonder!) People live in bodies! To prepare for sex by undressing and jumping into bed is to prepare *only* the body. But there is a live person in there who needs attention! It's the person living in that body with whom you must make love, not the body.

Sex, being more than physical, reflects the nature of God Himself in three ways. First: It reflects the personness of God as opposed to a force. God is not a force—He has personality. Man made in the image of God also has personality, as opposed to plants or animals which aren't created in God's image. There is a real significance about the face of man in the Bible. When God created Adam, He blew into the face of man. It's in the face of man that personality is reflected—His personness. Since man is the only creature made in the image of God, it isn't surprising that in some way man would be able to reflect God's image uniquely. The personness aspect of God's image is uniquely reflected as man and woman enjoy intercourse face-to-face. Only man procreates in this attitude.

Second: There is a reflection of another aspect of God's image —the plurality of persons. The animals were made out of the dust of the ground. God did something different with man. He made two out of one. Although a couple seeks oneness in their marriage, they are yet two distinct persons.

Third: There is a reflection of the union of the plurality of persons into one. Here we move in the other direction—toward oneness! It's that strange equation $1 + 1 = 1$. This reflects the trinitarian plurality, yet unity, aspect of God's image. In the Trinity the equation is $1 + 1 + 1 = 1$. God the Father + God the Son + God the Holy Spirit = One God! The marital relationship is also $1 + 1 + 1 = 1$: Man + Woman + God = One Maximum Marriage!

Sex, being more than physical, reflects the nature of God's relationship with man. Paul says, ". . . now I know in part, but then I shall know fully just as I also have been fully known" (1 Corinthians 13:12). God knows us thoroughly and intimately. In the meantime we are to set as our goal to "grow in the grace and knowledge of the Lord Jesus Christ" (*see* 2 Peter 3:18). Our relationship with God is to be characterized by this intimate, experiential knowledge of Him. The same is true of the husband-wife relationship. We are to set as our goal: to grow in the knowledge of one another. Man was designed for personal intimacy! The more your relationship is characterized by intimate knowledge of one another, the more it reflects the intimate relationship that is possible between man and God.

Another aspect of God's relationship with man that is reflected in sex is love by *covenant*. There are many ways of making a covenant with someone. You can shake hands on it. Can that be taken back? Sure! You can nullify it by shaking in reverse! The salt covenant was a method back in Bible times. To make a covenant with salt a person would take a pinch of salt out of his bag and place it in yours, and you would do the same to his bag. Can that be taken back? Certainly! If you could find the exact granules he put in your bag and you put in his, it couldn't be dissolved. Thankfully God didn't use either of these methods of making covenants. He used the blood covenant. The custom was to cut the sacrificial animals into two parts and lay the parts in parallel rows. Then the two parties would walk through the middle with arms clasped together. Can that be taken back? The only way it could be nullified was by the death of one of the parties. When God made a covenant with Abraham to set apart the Jewish people, He used this method. Only He altered it some. He put Abraham to sleep and walked through the middle of the animals Himself. Could this be taken back? Only if God dies! Since that is highly unlikely, this kind of covenant is an unconditional, permanent covenant of love. He used the same method—a blood covenant—when He sent His Son to die for the sins of the world. It was a permanent and unconditional expression of His love by covenant to us. Again your marital relationship is to reflect God's love relationship with man through your unconditional and permanent commitment of love by covenant to one another.

Sex, being more than physical, reflects the inner dimension of completeness. Are you excited and satisfied with the person who lives inside your mate's body? It will make all the difference in the world whether you enjoy sexual fulfillment in your marriage. There must be a mind-set, not on sex, but on the person—not on sexual performance, but on giving pleasure!

Sex Involves Body Ownership

It's interesting to see what God does to your body. He buys it and becomes the owner of your body. (*See* 1 Corinthians 6:19, 20.) When you get married He gives it away.

> Let the husband fulfill his duty to his wife, and likewise also the wife to her husband. The wife does not have authority over her own body, but the husband *does;* and likewise also the husband does not have authority over his own body, but the wife does.
>
> 1 Corinthians 7:3, 4

Carol and I have had lots of fun with that last verse. I say, "Body (which is her body, but I own it) come here!" She says, "Body (which is my body, but she owns it) go into the kitchen!" You could never get together that way! Paul continues:

> Stop depriving one another, except by agreement for a time that you may devote yourselves to prayer, and come together again lest Satan tempt you because of your lack of self-control.
>
> 1 Corinthians 7:5

The issue is not "how often" you make love, but that you are always ready to please your mate—"fulfill your duty" (v. 3). I'll never forget sitting in a seminar where the speaker gave the "national average" of lovemaking per week. After he gave it, couples looked at each other in utter amazement. Some felt as if they were "hyper" and others checked their pulse to see if they were still alive! The so-called national average has nothing to do with your relationship. The real importance is that you're meeting one another's needs sexually.

Now when you really don't feel like making love with your mate, meet your mate's needs by anticipation. There are certainly genuine reasons for not making love. When I finish speaking at a Maximum Marriage Seminar, I'm too tired to pucker—let alone make love! Let's say your wife wants to make love some evening and you really don't feel like it. Here's what you do. Tell her, "Honey, I'll tell you what, tomorrow night let's make it a special time together. I'll be sure to function as head during the 'valley of the shadow'; we'll get the kids to bed early, and then we'll be alone to enjoy one another." The next morning as you leave for work you give her a kiss. Not a peck on the cheek, but a real kiss—one that says, I wish I didn't have to leave you. Then rush off to work! (That's important!) That afternoon give your wife a call expressing your enthusiasm about the coming evening together. Then hang up—don't talk too long! Pick up some flowers on the way home—maybe one for each of the years you've known her. (For some, that could get expensive—divide by three!) When you are finally alone, you will not believe the beautiful response from your wife. Why? Because you built her mind-set through anticipation.

Be careful of lame excuses. Solomon came to Shulamit's door late at night, wanting to make love. (See 5:2, 3.) In this case the "King" really did arrive home; but he made the same move that men have been famous for over the centuries—the late-night approach. Although his timing was wrong, Shulamit still shouldn't have given the two lame excuses:

> SOLOMON: Open to me, my sister, my darling,
> My dove, my perfect one!
> For my head is drenched with dew,
> My locks with the damp of the night.

> SHULAMIT: I have taken off my dress,
> How can I put it on again?

Can't you just visualize Solomon in his frustration. He was probably thinking, *So why do you need to put your dress on?*

> SHULAMIT: I have washed my feet,
> How can I dirty them again?

Now she's getting religious on him! The ancients practiced a ceremonial washing of the feet before going to bed. Both of her excuses are pretty weak!

One husband wrote to his wife in jest, surfacing the issue of rejection through lame excuses:

To My Loving Wife,

During the past year I have tried to make love to you 365 times. I have succeeded only thirty-six times; this is an average of once every ten days. The following is a list of the reasons why I did not succeed more often: It was too late, too early, too hot, or too cold. It would waken the children, the company in the next room, or the neighbors whose windows were open. You were too full; or you had a headache, backache, toothache, or the giggles. You pretended to be asleep or were not in the mood. You had on your mudpack. You watched the late TV show; I watched the late TV show; or the baby was crying.

During the times I did succeed the activity was not entirely satisfactory for a variety of reasons. Six times you chewed gum the whole time; on occasion you watched TV the whole time. Often you told me to hurry up and get it over with. A few times I tried to waken you to tell you we were through; and one time I was afraid I had hurt you for I felt you move.

Honey, it's no wonder I drink too much.

YOUR LOVING HUSBAND

You are responsible for meeting your mate's needs sexually. That may not mean just making love. It may mean showing affection verbally and physically at times other than when in bed. Obviously you must use discretion before the children. However, they need models of a love relationship, and they need to know that mommy and daddy are excited about one another.

God gives so much freedom in lovemaking. Because people carry over into marriage the connotation that there is something dirty or ungodly about sex many limitations are placed upon the sexual relationship. It's clear in the Bible that there are no limits outside of two qualifications: the first is that your mate's needs must be met, and the second is that whatever is done must be done by mutual consent. (See 1 Corinthians 7:3, 5.) What a fantastic freedom for a full expression of your love!

Sex Is Being Open Physically and Emotionally

In Genesis 2:25 we find the first married couple naked and not ashamed. They had total communication without inhibitions— physically (naked) and emotionally (not ashamed). Then later in Genesis 3 the two no longer are experiencing the openness they once enjoyed. Now they're hunting for fig leaves to hide from God and from one another. What has caused this sudden change from a cheerful open relationship to one that is dismally closed? In this case the answer is obvious: The fall of man occurs. Man is in rebellion to God. It's sin! Since the fall our world is sick with rebellion and violation of God's principles. Therefore our marriages suffer because we are closed from God and from one another—hunting for fig leaves. God intended the marital relationship to be open and free. Though it's a struggle, you must continually fight that which closes your relationship and pursue the openness God designed.

I'm amazed at the openness displayed by Solomon and Shulamit! They are absolutely excited about one another physically and emotionally. This excitement is present not only at first in their marriage (as would be expected) but also later on. You would think, from the way they talk to one another, that he is Mr. Atlas and she's Miss America. But I doubt that either of them would be that appealing to many of you today. For example, in praising his love Solomon says, "Your belly is like a heap of wheat" (see 7:2). When I first read that I thought he must mean that her belly is yellow like wheat. After studying the Song, I realize he's not saying "heap of *wheat*," but "*heap* of wheat," meaning her belly stuck out a little.

It wasn't that Solomon and Shulamit were such "beautiful people," but that they were beautiful to one another. Each was totally excited about the other's body; each saw nothing unclean or inadequate about any part of the other's body. Are you excited and satisfied with your mate's body? Are you willing to receive your mate's body as from God? Have you told him/her so?

Sex Requires Verbalization

For maximum sexual enjoyment your relationship needs the verbal reassurance and affirmation of love. Let's listen in on Solomon and Shulamit on their wedding night (4:1–7).

> SOLOMON: How beautiful you are, my darling,
> How beautiful you are!

> Your eyes are like doves behind your veil;
> Your hair is like a flock of goats
> That have descended from Mount Gilead.

Here he goes again! Her "hair is like a flock of goats." He's saying that her hair is long, black, and flowing like a flock of goats as they descend the mountain.

> SOLOMON: Your teeth are like a flock of newly shorn ewes
> Which have come up from their washing,

He's saying her teeth are beautifully white. Now some of you won't be able to take the next couplet.

> All of which bear twins,
> And not one among them has lost her young.

All of her teeth are twins; they come in pairs, top and bottom, and are evenly matched. Not only that, but she still had all her teeth (had lost none of her young). That could be a little tough on some people. (One woman in the seminar said, "I've got all my teeth; they're just in the jar at home!")

> SOLOMON: Your lips are like a scarlet thread,
> And your mouth is lovely.
> Your temples are like a slice of a pomegranate
> Behind your veil.
> Your neck is like the tower of David
> Built with rows of stones,
> On which are hung a thousand shields,
> All the round shields of the mighty men.

Her rosy cheeks resemble the pomegranate when cut open. Her queenly stature spoke to him of inner strength. She held herself well.

> Your two breasts are like two fawns,
> Twins of a gazelle,
> Which feed among the lilies.
> Until the cool of the day

> When the shadows flee away,
> I will go my way to the mountain of myrrh
> And to the hill of frankincense.
> You are altogether beautiful, my darling,
> And there is no blemish in you.

And they consummate their love for each other.
Shulamit verbalizes her love and excitement for Solomon too
(5:10–14).

> SHULAMIT: My beloved is dazzling and ruddy,
> Outstanding among ten thousand.
> His head is like gold, pure gold;
> His locks are like clusters of dates,
> And black as a raven.
> His eyes are like doves,
> Beside streams of water,
> Bathed in milk,
> And reposed in their setting.
> His cheeks are like a bed of balsam,
> Banks of sweet-scented herbs;
> His lips are lilies,
> Dripping with liquid myrrh.
> His hands are rods of gold
> Set with beryl;
> His abdomen is carved ivory
> Inlaid with sapphires.

Her remarks about his abdomen being carved ivory seem to
indicate that his stomach was firm. In other words, he wasn't
suffering from "Dunlap's" disease—*duh* belly *dun* lapped over
duh belt!
In addition to the freedom of verbalizing positive excitement
about your mate, there should be a freedom to verbalize specific
instructions. Shulamit gives specific instructions to Solomon as
to what she would like him to do in their lovemaking (2:4–6).

> SHULAMIT: He has brought me to his banquet hall,
> And his banner over me is love.
> Sustain me with raisin cakes,

> Refresh me with apples,
> Because I am lovesick.
> Let his left hand be under my head
> And his right hand embrace me.

Notice that all of her instructions are positive. When a mate is trying hard to please the other, a negative Don't! or No! crushes the person. Be more positive! Communicate pleasure and enjoyment with positive instructions like: "Do this or that!" or "Touch me here!"

Sex Is a Priority—That Takes Time

So take time! Solomon's late-night approach and the typical "ten-minute quickie" allow little time for enjoyment or communication.

Sex is not to be an afterthought but demands forethought. In our pressurized world a two-week vacation, once a year, is a meager relief from the stress and tension of life. Why not plan frequent getaways! They don't have to be expensive, but an extended time together can be extremely significant in building and maintaining a oneness factor in your marriage. Take Song of Solomon along with you! Read the Song together—the husband can read Solomon's part and the wife can read Shulamit's. (The New American Standard Bible has an excellent margin guide showing the division of the speakers in the Song.) The first time you read through just discuss what they're saying. The second reading might be the real thing—where you both are speaking your parts to one another, expressing excitement and appreciation of the other. Now there is a third part in the Song; it's the CHORUS. It's not really a chorus, but a literary device for changing scenes. So don't feel compelled to take anyone with you on your getaway! As you read the Song to one another you're well on your way to making love by use of the Bible. It's biblical lovemaking! It's the most intimate expression of a maximum marriage—the consummation of a full reflection of God's image.

IV

Disorder or Design?

10

God Designed the Family—
He Can Make It Work

For one to fully comprehend God's design for marriage and to be excited about it, some questions must be answered: Why the design? Why marriage? and Why the Designer? Now that marriage has been in existence a few thousand years, someone ought to let the secret out. Is the purpose only to produce children? There certainly must be a better reason for marriage than that. Why should two people enter into a lifelong relationship just for procreation?

Why the Design?

Then God said, "Let Us make man in Our image, according to Our likeness; and let them rule over the fish of the sea and over the birds of the sky and over the cattle and over all the earth, and over every creeping thing that creeps on the earth." And God created man in His own image, in the image of God He created him; male and female He created them. And God blessed them; and God said to them, "Be fruitful and multiply, and fill the earth, and subdue it; and rule over the fish of the sea and over the birds of the sky, and over every living thing that moves on the earth." Then God said, "Behold, I have given you every plant yielding seed that is on the surface of all the earth, and every tree which has fruit yielding seed; it shall be food for you; and to every beast of the earth and to every bird of the sky and to every thing that moves on the earth which has life, I have given every green plant for food"; and it was so. And God saw all that He had made, and behold, it was very good. And there was evening and there was morning, the sixth day.

Genesis 1:26–31

At this point in the history of the world, Lucifer, "star of the morning," had already staged a rebellion against God in order to set himself up as sovereign ruler of the universe. For this God cast him out of heaven to the earth (Isaiah 14:12–17; Ezekiel 28:11–19). Thus the earth was Satan's domain at the time of man's creation, and it remains so now (2 Corinthians 4:4; Ephesians 2:2; Luke 4:5–7). The fact that Satan was "alive and well on planet earth" significantly affects the understanding of the purpose behind God's creation of the first family unit.

Generally the Lord seems to view man as His offensive force to planet earth, His intention is eventually to take back the earth from Satan. Donald Grey Barnhouse in his book *The Invisible War* expresses what seems to be God's edict:

> "We shall give this rebellion a thorough trial. We shall permit it to run its full course. The universe shall see what a creature, though he be the highest creature ever to spring from God's Word, can do apart from Him. We shall watch this experiment, and permit the universe of creatures to watch it, during this brief interlude between eternity past and eternity future called time. In it the spirit of independence shall be allowed to expand to the utmost. And the wreck and ruin which shall result will demonstrate to the universe, and forever, that there is no life, no joy, no peace apart from a complete dependence upon the Most High God, Possessor of heaven and earth."

Marital conflict is not just a battle between husband and wife, but is a critical part of the spiritual battle of the heavenlies between God and Satan.

Why Marriage?

There appear to be three purposes for God's primary offensive force—the marital union: to reflect the image of God; to reproduce godly children, and to reign together.

> And God created man in His own image, in the image of God He created him; male and female He created them.
>
> Genesis 1:27

It is through the oneness of the male-female relationship that the image of God is most fully reflected. Notice that it is not the man or the woman alone who reflects the image of God, but the oneness of the man *and* woman. Man cannot reflect God's image alone. Woman cannot reflect God's image alone. It is most fully expressed through the $1 + 1 = 1$ relationship of marriage. The norm for man and woman is marriage. (There are obvious exceptions—for example, the spiritual gift of celibacy. In this particular case where God has led a person to be single He will certainly complete the reflection of His image in that person Himself.) Within the context of Satan's domain God desires that His image be reflected to the world as a light in a dark room.

The most substantial reflection of the image of God was the God-man—Jesus Christ. Paul tells us, "He is the image of the invisible God" (*see* Colossians 1:15). We are constantly exhorted to be imitators of Christ, to be conformed into the image of Christ, or to be Christlike. Even though God has given us everything with which to live the Christlike life, we are to diligently and consistently walk in our newness of life. As Jesus said, this is not the broad road which is easy to walk, but the narrow road which is difficult. If the marital relationship is going to be a Christlike reflection (the image of God), then it must be a relationship of mutual encouragement and edification toward this goal. Unfortunately, because of the popular power struggle most marriages are the exact opposite—discouragement and destruction.

The second purpose of God's design is to reproduce godly children: "Be fruitful and multiply, and fill the earth" (*see* Genesis 1:28). What a familiar statement! Yet it is so misunderstood concerning its impact. His point was not just that mankind should reproduce. This command was given for the purpose of rearing children toward *godliness* and filling the earth with godly people. Why? To counteract the spirit of ungodliness which came about as a result of Satan's fall.

The third purpose of God's design is that man and woman might reign together in God's kingdom upon this earth. The man and the woman were given the command to rule over "everything that moves on the earth which has life" (*see* Genesis 1:28–30).

Then God gave them more specific instructions concerning the garden. The garden became their local sphere of the world. They were to cultivate and keep it (*see* Genesis 2:15). The word *cultivate,* as translated, literally means to labor, work, or serve. It is the normal word used for service to God. The emphasis here is not so much on the *garden* as it is on the *services* of the two in the garden. God could just as easily have placed them in a garment factory or on a cattle ranch. He was most interested in their service and conduct before Him in the sphere of the garden. The word rendered *keep* means to watch, guard, or preserve. They were to be careful to guard the garden from being anything other than what God intended. They needed to watch out for any problems within the garden (their own conduct) and for any problems outside the garden (which might alter what God had established there).

In reigning together in God's kingdom on this earth the husband-wife team must "cultivate and keep" their local sphere of influence. The Christian life of service for God is to be lived together, deriving strength from one another—God intended a team effort. Anything other than this must be second best. However, it isn't merely growing and serving the Lord together (*cultivating*). That is just one side of the coin; the other side is to *keep* or to *guard.* Today the marriage relationship still exists to stand against the spiritual forces of evil. Satan's kingdom is defeated as husband and wife join in spiritual battle by depending together on the Lord and resisting the devil. This is what James refers to when he says, "Submit therefore to God [that is, *cultivate*—serve]. Resist the devil and he will flee from you" [that is, *keep* guard] (James 4:7). Satan concentrates his major attacks on the marriage relationship because he knows that a couple living by God's principles is his greatest enemy. So the male-female relationship is one of ministering and working toward making an impact upon the world for God as a *team*—not as individuals—*reigning together.*

God designed marriage to reflect His image, to reproduce godly children, and to reign together. Since God designed the family, He *can* make it work through His principles. Biblical principles are *living* principles. Even if you do not understand them, they are always true. I do not understand how electricity works, but I use it constantly. I do not understand how a brown cow can eat green grass and produce white milk and yellow butter, but I eat all of these (except the grass). The law of gravity predicts that every time a man steps off of a two-story building he will go down fast, hit with a thud, and will not like it. Some principles are always true no matter what our responses may be to them.

As we examine various principles relating to the marriage union it will be extremely easy to write some off as ridiculous or to ignore them altogether. But no matter how you respond, these principles are true; it is only within the principles of God's design for marriage that real hope for oneness lies.

Why the Designer?

The principles of God's design are true and they work, but it is virtually impossible to take part in the design without knowing the Designer personally and committing yourself to Him. God, the Designer, created us in such a way that we can function maximally as individuals only if He is a vital part of our lives. This brings us to the question: Why the Designer? Why is it necessary for God to be a part of the *Maximum Marriage?* There are two very important reasons why this commitment to God, the Designer, is necessary within the marriage bond.

The first reason is to prevent conflict through the uniting of two different natures.   Paul refers to this in 2 Corinthians: "Do not be bound together with unbelievers; for what fellowship has light with darkness? . . . or what has a believer in common with an unbeliever?" (*see* 6:14, 15). The idea behind this passage is found in the Old Testament law which says not to plow with an ox and a donkey together (Deuteronomy 22:10). Why? Because they have two completely different natures. When one wants to go the other will sit down, and you will never get your work done! The same is true with people. Man from birth possesses a nature that is basically self-centered. It is bent toward self-gratification and away from God; it's an "optical" problem—the big *I*. When a person comes into a relationship with the personal God, his nature is changed; he is given a new nature that is bent toward God and derives its strength from Him. Paul's warning is not to join a believer (a God-centered nature) and an unbeliever (a self-centered nature). The result would be discord and disharmony—a lack of communication. The two different natures would prevent them from moving toward the oneness that was intended. So both the husband and the wife need a change of nature—a change from being self-centered to being God-centered.

In order to prevent conflict in your marriage you must take some action. You need a change of nature. It is in man's spirit that such a change occurs. Jesus used birth as an illustration of this point. He said, "That which is born of the flesh is flesh [physical birth]; and that which is born of the Spirit is spirit [spiritual birth]" (John 3:6). Just as it was necessary for you to be born physically in order to enter a relationship with the physical realm, so is it necessary for you to be born spiritually in order to enter into a relationship with God in the spiritual realm.

There are actually two ways to have a relationship with God. The first is to be perfect. If you are perfect, then you don't have a nature that is bent toward self and away from God. The self-centered nature produces rebellion against God and His principles. The common attitude toward God is: God, you go your way and I'll go mine. Check with me when I'm seventy-two or seventy-three and we'll negotiate! This rebellion is what the Bible calls *sin*. Now if you don't have such a nature you will not need the spiritual birth. While you are examining yourself for perfection, however, let me insert a thought. Paul says, "There is none righteous [perfect], not even one; . . . for all have sinned and fall short of the glory of God" (*see* Romans 3:10, 23). Now that your potential for perfection has been obliterated we can progress to the second way to have a relationship with God. It is at this point that spiritual birth becomes a necessity. Spiritual birth is simple. Since everyone has a self-centered nature that is contrary to God and His Word, then everyone needs a new nature that is alive toward God. This new nature can only be obtained by spiritual birth. God makes it clear that He demands a payment for our sin against Him—death. Either you can attempt to pay for it yourself by dying for eternity or you can accept God's payment through the death of His Son, Jesus Christ. The moment a person realizes that his sin must be paid for and accepts God's payment, the Lord creates within him a new nature that is bent toward God and enables him to live by God's principles. "Therefore if any man is in Christ, *he is* a new creature; the old things passed away; behold, new things have come" (2 Corinthians 5:17).

Bob walked into my office filled with despair concerning his marriage and life in general. He said, "I've heard a little of what you say about marriage and I'm convinced that my wife can't do any of it! She's a zero!" I asked, "Well, what about you?" He said, "Oh, I'm pretty bad off myself, but not quite as bad as she is!" I continued to press him on his responsibility in the marriage. Finally, he said, "Look, for my wife and me to get this thing together, we'd have to be turned inside out!" What Bob was saying was significant. He saw clearly that they had no capacity to experience God's design together. They needed a new capacity to live life. They both needed a changed nature. That day Bob trusted in Jesus Christ's payment for his sin. Even though he was a "new creature" with a new nature, he, as with every human being, could not get rid of his old self-centered nature. The Christian life then becomes a process of growth whereby one learns to walk more consistently in his new nature and to reject his old nature. So when Bob arrived home that evening, he didn't sprout wings nor was he perfect. Yet his wife sensed something was different and she liked it. A few days later she called in and said, "I don't know what Bob got over there, but can I come in and get the same dose?" She came in and "got the same dose." Bob and Jean are now able to experience the design for marital oneness, because they both came into a personal relationship with God, the Designer.

The second reason you must commit yourself to God is to promote communication through mutual submission to God as the Designer of the marriage.   The Apostle John expressed the general principle this way: "but if we walk in the light as He Himself is in the light, we have fellowship with one another, and the blood of Jesus His Son cleanses us from all sin" (1 John 1:7). This is not specifically speaking to the marital relationship, but certainly can be applied to it as with all relationships. If a husband and wife walk in the light, the result is fellowship with one another. The word *fellowship* is a beautiful term meaning to share intimately and take part in—communication. What marriage is not looking for that? Lack of communication is the greatest problem in marriage today. This verse says that communication can be yours, if you walk in the light.

What does it mean to walk in the light? To walk in the light is to submit yourself to God and His principles. This can be an uncomfortable experience, because the light exposes all the dirt—the defeats and failures. Often I vacuum the house for my wife. In order to make it exciting, I sometimes time myself—trying for a new record! On one occasion I was moving along quite swiftly. It looked like I was performing in record time. As I progressed up the hallway I came to my study off to the right. I'm very familiar with my study. I've spent a lot of time there. So in my attempt for the new vacuuming record I decided to quickly sweep through the study without turning on the light. My strategy paid off! I beat my best time by a good ten seconds. As usual my wife walked through the house for inspection. I'll never forget what she said as she looked into my study. "Honey, it looks like you didn't turn the light on in here!" What was her first clue? The dirt on the carpet that I missed in my haste. When you turn the light on, it will expose the dirt. The same is true when walking into God's light. The gap between what He says to do and what is actually going on can be overwhelming!

There is something different about God's light; it not only exposes the dirt, the shortcomings, but it removes the dirt as well. Two people desiring to have maximum communication in their marital relationship can start all over as they walk into God's light. Resentment and hatred so easily strangle the very life out of a marriage. There must be a solution whereby that resentment and hatred are dissolved, where husband and wife can experience true forgiveness within their relationship. This happens as the couple begins walking in the light, first experiencing God's forgiveness and then the capacity to forgive one another.

The practical step here is to invite the Lord to be the Designer of your marriage. Submit yourself to Him and to His principles.

Walk in the light! The result? Oneness—oneness by design. That is maximum marriage!

If God designed the family, can He make it work? Well, God designed the family to reflect His Image to the world, to reproduce godly children, and to reign together in the spiritual warfare. Since He designed the family, He can make it work. But He can't make it work without you!

James 1:22 warns us not to be merely hearers of the Word, who delude ourselves into thinking we have it because we've heard it. The goal is to be doers of the Word. I've discussed at length God's game plan for a maximum marriage. Now it's your turn to translate these principles into the blood and guts of personal application.

We often hear these words which offer a serious challenge: **"If Christianity doesn't work in the home, maybe it really doesn't work at all!"**